Series / Number 07-058

RANDOMIZED RESPONSE

A Method for Sensitive Surveys

D1218094

JAMES ALAN FOX
PAUL E. TRACY
Northeastern University

SAGE PUBLICATIONS
The International Professional Publishers
Newbury Park   London   New Delhi

11-8-95

For information address:

SAGE Publications, Inc.
2455 Teller Road
Newbury Park, California 91320

SAGE Publications Ltd.
6 Bonhill Street
London EC2A 4PU
United Kingdom

SAGE Publications India Pvt. Ltd.
M-32 Market
Greater Kailash I
New Delhi 110 048 India

International Standard Book Number 0-8039-2309-0

Library of Congress Catalog Card No. 85-063713

95 96 97 98 99 10 9 8 7 6

When citing a university paper, please use the proper form. Remember to cite the correct
Sage University Paper series title and include the paper number. One of the following
formats can be adapted (depending on the style manual used):

(1) IVERSEN, GUDMUND R. and NORPOTH, HELMUT (1976) "Analysis of
Variance." Sage University Paper series on Quantitative Applications in the Social
Sciences, 07-001. Beverly Hills: Sage Pubns.

OR

(2) Iversen, Gudmund R. and Norpoth, Helmut. 1976. *Analysis of Variance.* Sage
University Paper series on Quantitative Applications in the Social Sciences, series no.
07-001. Beverly Hills: Sage Pubns.

CONTENTS

The New York Times – Carnegie Hall Poll

Series Editor's Introduction

Survey research is useful for studying a wide variety of problems. Suppose, however, that one wished to do a survey about the spread of AIDS, the incidence of abortions among teenagers, the frequency of spouse beatings, or any other such subject. One approach would be to ask respondents directly about these controversial topics. But can a researcher expect to get honest answers? Can we get good estimates of behavioral frequencies when the behavior is severely disapproved and perhaps even criminal?

The answer is that we *can* get good information, but not by naively asking respondents to report attitudes and behaviors that might land them in jail. In *Randomized Response*, James Alan Fox and Paul E. Tracy describe an innovative survey method designed for sensitive or threatening inquiries. In the first part of the monograph, Fox and Tracy discuss the sources of error in surveys, especially in responses to sensitive, socially disapproved, or incriminating behaviors and attitudes. They then discuss the traditional strategies for protecting the anonymity of respondents and the confidentiality of responses, noting that these protections are either limited or at least perceived by respondents to be ineffective.

The bulk of the volume concentrates on describing the randomized response method and how it can be used effectively and efficiently to protect survey respondents and thereby minimize survey bias. The authors show how randomized response can be employed to estimate parameters of both qualitative and quantitative measures, to test subgroup differences, and to perform bivariate and multivariate analyses. They pay particular attention to survey design considerations and include sample questions and research examples.

Their presentation of the applications of randomized response indicates that this approach can be utilized fruitfully in a variety of disciplines and substantive contexts. Their careful exposition of all aspects of the method lays a firm foundation for the reader to apply the technique whenever the research is sensitive and concerns about

5

anonymity and confidentiality are paramount. More generally, the Fox and Tracy volume will make randomized response a more widely understood and accepted procedure, thereby reducing what is often a hindrance to the use of surveys on controversial topics.

—Richard G. Niemi
Series Co-Editor

RANDOMIZED RESPONSE

A Method for Sensitive Surveys

JAMES ALAN FOX
PAUL E. TRACY
Northeastern University

1. SURVEYING SENSITIVE TOPICS

The social survey has become one of the foremost tools for collecting information concerning human populations. It has proven to be extremely useful for measuring opinions, attitudes, and behaviors that span a broad spectrum of interest. The need for survey methods is clear in several respects.

First and most obvious is the fact that certain kinds of data are not available in archival records. In criminology, for example, information concerning undetected crime and unreported victimization experiences is absent from official crime records. Second, owing to privacy and security concerns, some records are inaccessible to researchers. In most if not all states, access to criminal history data of specific persons is generally prohibited by statute. Third, there are often logistical problems surrounding the use of records. The study population may be so geographically dispersed that the use of records may not be feasible. Last, archival research can often be very expensive and exceedingly time-consuming.

For these and a host of other reasons, the survey method is often the preferred choice for studying certain phenomena. In some disciplines it can even be considered a mandatory tool of the trade. The survey method, however, is not without problems. One area of concern is the reliability and validity of survey data owing to response effects and other measurement problems. More and more literature is now being devoted to methodological treatments of interview method and questionnaire design.[1] Additionally, as surveys have become more and more prevalent and have involved larger and larger segments of the population, there is growing concern over the ethical and legal implications of surveying human populations.

These concerns become critical when survey respondents are asked extremely sensitive, embarrassing, threatening, or even incriminating questions. Even when the researcher goes to great lengths to guarantee the security of respondents' answers, subjects can be skeptical and may be reluctant to supply truthful replies. Aside from the crucial issue of the validity of sensitive inquiries, ethical and legal considerations are equally paramount. That is, the need for research on sensitive phenomena must be balanced against the right of human subjects to privacy. This issue is made more acute by the potential misuse of sensitive data by the research community.

We identify the kinds of measurement problems customary in survey research. We also describe the ethical and legal problems inherent in surveying human subjects. Last, we discuss the traditional approaches that have been adopted to minimize these problems.

Types of Error in Surveys

Survey estimates are subject to two main sources of error (see Figure 1). The first, sampling error, arises from the variation that is present because a segment or sample is studied instead of a complete enumeration of the population. Sampling error can be remediated in several ways. Different sampling designs can be employed which increase the representativeness of the sample. Complex estimation procedures have also been developed to minimize sampling error and improve the efficiency of survey estimates.

The second type of error, nonsampling error, is much more problematic.[2] When respondents are surveyed about their opinions, attitudes, behaviors, and the like, nonsampling error can in turn be of two types. One type is random error, which reduces the reliability of measurements. Random errors can be expected to cancel out over repeated measurements. The other type of nonsampling error is nonrandom and thus constitutes bias in survey data. Bias, or systematic error, can have several sources, but our concern here is with two major sources.

One source of bias in surveys is subjects' refusal to respond, called "nonresponse bias." Bias arises due to differences between respondents

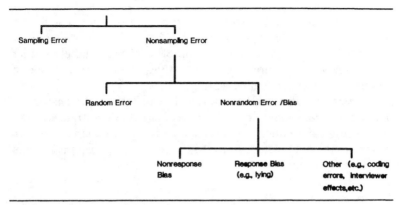

Figure 1: Types of Survey Error

who do and do not respond to survey questions. When these differences are related to criterion measures, the results may be misleading or even erroneous. In addition, the variance of the estimates becomes greater as the size of the sample is reduced by refusals to respond. Consequently, confidence limits are more difficult to construct and the size of the intervals increases concomitant with the degree of nonresponse.

Another source of bias is response error arising from the deliberate falsification of information. Systematic distortion of the respondent's true status jeopardizes the validity of survey measurements. Unlike random error, response bias does not cancel out over repeated measurements. Rather, the distortion between a respondent's true and observed scores persists.

Phillips (1971) has shown that the problem of response bias is likely to arise even in surveys of relatively innocuous information, owing in part to a respondent's perceptions and needs which can emerge during the data collection process. Thus the potential for bias to arise in surveys of sensitive information can be considered particularly troublesome due to heightened respondent concern over anonymity. Specifically, the varying tendencies among respondents in sensitive surveys to cooperate in the first instance, or to underreport/overreport if they agree to respond at all, can lead to erroneous estimates concerning the extent and correlates of the sensitive phenomena under study.

Systematic response error—both nonresponse and response biases—is a serious threat to survey research. It can vitiate the method in which respondents' reports are frequently the best or the only way to gather certain kinds of data. Nevertheless, a review of survey research on a particularly sensitive topic—criminal behavior—indicates that few researchers have acknowledged the problem of bias, and even fewer have employed appropriate techniques to estimate the magnitude of bias and its effects on findings (Bridges, 1979).

It seems clear that neglect of this and related issues has delayed the development and adoption of alternate data-gathering strategies. The perpetuation of traditional survey methods is problematic because such methods may not be at all suited to the collection of certain kinds of information from particular classes of respondents.

Ethical Issues in Surveys

When all the rationales and justifications for its use have been stripped away, the social survey is ultimately an intrusion into the private lives of individuals. In a most comprehensive treatment of the ethical issues that arise in survey research methods,[3] Boruch and Cecil (1979: 3) state: "Sharing one's thoughts, attitudes and experiences with a social researcher can be regarded, in principle, as a depreciation of privacy."

In a recent monograph on survey methods, Sudman and Bradburn (1982) have shown that ethical problems in surveys tend to center on three principles. First, when individuals are selected to participate in a survey, their privacy has been violated. This "right to privacy" includes not only the respondent's behavior but also his or her attitudes, opinions, and beliefs. According to Sudman and Bradburn, the right to privacy is not absolute, as the interests of society may sometimes justify a privacy violation. Rather, the right to privacy should generally be under the control of the individual.

The second principle involves the issue of confidentiality. When a researcher agrees to keep survey data confidential, he or she cannot pass this information on to other persons. In other words, survey data that have been obtained under an assurance that they will be kept secret *must* be kept secret (Sudman and Bradburn, 1982: 8).

The final ethical principle identified by Sudman and Bradburn concerns "informed consent." "Potential respondents should be given sufficient information about what they are actually being asked and the uses to which it will be put—to judge whether unpleasant consequences will follow as a result of disclosure" (Sudman and Bradburn, 1982: 8-9). Most survey respondents are not at risk and can expect few if any unwanted consequences as a result of their participation. For these persons, informed consent is not very problematic. But what of respondents who are asked to report sensitive, even illegal, behaviors?

Some of these respondents may experience nothing more than personal embarrassment or short-lived anxiety during questioning. Other respondents may be stigmatized by neighbors, friends, and others should the sensitive data become known. In some cases, respondents could face more severe risks, such as prosecution, should the data be made available to authorities. Clearly, respondents face differential risks and should be informed accordingly. One can only surmise what effect this will have on respondents who are not given sufficient assurances that they will be protected, or who do not trust that such assurances will work as promised.

Boruch and Cecil (1979) have persuasively argued that the essential problem concerns adherence to ethical standards without, at the same time, drastically constraining the research process. Respondents must be protected; it is the researcher's responsibility to do so. However, it is equally clear that methods of respecting a respondent's privacy, and above all ensuring that his or her answers will remain confidential, vary in their consequences for the research process. These costs can be negligible, while others have nontrivial methodological and statistical consequences. On this point Boruch and Cecil (1979: 6) state:

> Our goal is to minimize identifiability of response, under the constraint that research itself must not be degraded intolerably by the process. This sets one value, individual privacy, as paramount, but under the constraint, research standards are only a bit less important.

This equation of respondent protection versus the need for research is further complicated by the fact that assurances of confidentiality can be destroyed in the face of forced disclosure of research data. Boruch (1972) was one of the first to comment on the possibility that researchers in some disciplines may be threatened with the appropriation of their data for use in civil or criminal actions brought against the respondents. When the issue is forced disclosure under a subpoena, Baruch and Cecil (1979: 25-26) argue: "The researcher may find it impossible to abide by both the promise of confidentiality made to a respondent and the demands of a court, legislative committee, or executive agency for information about identified respondents." A researcher may find it difficult to resist these demands for the data because litigation will be costly and time-consuming, contempt citations could result in imprisonment, and, in the case of information on criminal activity, the researcher could be charged with conspiracy and with being an accessory after the fact.

In the final analysis, therefore, methods to protect human subjects must not only ensure confidentiality to the satisfaction of the subject without greatly affecting the design and conduct of the research but must also be sufficiently effective or powerful to withstand attempts to appropriate the data and to buffer the researcher from outside interference.

Respondent Protections

LEGAL METHODS

One way in which researchers can protect respondents is through legal means. Boruch and Cecil (1979) identify three such means: executive discretion, judicial control over the admissibility of evidence, and legislative protection. Before discussing the specific features of these methods, it should be noted that, as a class, they are limited in their scope and range of applicability.

Executive discretion involves an officer of government promising that research can occur without fear of subpoena or other government interference. Such executive orders can occur at the federal, state, and local levels. Boruch and Cecil (1979: 230-231) note several problems with this procedure: law enforcement officials must cooperate; when the research extends across jurisdictions, multiple agreements are necessary; and federal guidelines can be ignored at the local level. For these reasons, executive discretion will be an important source of protection for certain high-visibility studies but not for the broad spectrum of social research.

Judicial protection is possible in a number of ways. The judiciary may recognize the subject-researcher relationship as privileged. Research data can be viewed as protected by the Constitution since, if researchers were forced to reveal data, other research would be compromised, thus restricting the free flow of information which is protected by the First Amendment. Last, because the judiciary has discretion over the admissibility of evidence at trial, courts can balance the need for the research data as evidence against the public interest in maintaining confidentiality between researchers and their sources.

Research data can also be protected by statute. A number of federal statutes have been passed which severely restrict, if not prohibit, access to research data identifiable to specific respondents. For example, the Public Health Services Act as amended in 1974 [Pub. L. 93-282 at 42 U.S.C.A. para. 242(a)], the Controlled Substances Act [Pub. L. 91-513 at 21 U.S.C.A. para. 872(c)], the Drug Abuse Office and Treatment Act of 1972 as amended in 1974 [Pub. L. 93-282 at 21 U.S.C.A. para. 1175(a)], and the Crime Control Act of 1973 [Pub. L. 93-83 at 42 U.S.C.A. para. 3771] are federal statutes which authorize researchers to withhold the names of subjects, thus making the data immune to legal process.

Boruch and Cecil (1979) argue that statutory protection is preferable to judicial or executive action because it offers more uniformity. Further, executive protections and judicial exclusions are often discretionary, can be invoked only on a case-by-case basis, and have occurred only sparingly. Despite their uniformity and authority, current statutory protections are restricted to certain kinds of research and are limited in the scope of protections given. Topics such as drug and alcohol abuse, crime and delinquency, and physical and mental health are protected by statute when federal funding is involved. When such funding is absent, or when economic, educational, political, psychological, and sociological research topics are involved, no statutory protections are readily available. Thus most social science research is conducted outside the realm of statutory protection.

PROTECTION THROUGH ANONYMITY

Beyond the legal methods, which we have seen are limited either by their unlikely availability or by their narrow scope, is the more familiar and conventional approach to protecting respondents—anonymous data collection. This approach can take the form of a self-administered questionnaire, a telephone survey, or a mail questionnaire, to name the most common techniques. Each of these methods is used in place of the face-to-face interview to protect respondents and to reduce the threat of sensitive questions by granting the subject anonymity. (Also, these strategies are far less expensive than the face-to-face interview.) The respondent simply supplies the requested survey data without any personal identifiers.

Despite the simplicity and apparent advantages of these methods (the self-administered questionnaire, in particular, which some researchers have claimed to be optimal; see, for example, Sudman and Bradburn,

1974: 142-143; Hardt and Peterson-Hardt, 1977: 257), there are important limitations. Some of these relate to respondent concerns, while others involve the research capabilities themselves.

Although self-administered questionnaires given in a group setting or by mail are anonymous, respondents may believe that identifiers (e.g., pinholes or secret codes) exist on the forms which can somehow link the data to them. When a group setting is not possible, a questionnaire can be administered to respondents individually. However, to the respondent this process can have some of the markings of a personal interview in terms of perceived level of anonymity. Similarly, even when phone surveys are accomplished through random dialing to produce anonymity, respondents may believe that the researcher has recorded the number and can trace the data back to particular subjects.

These methods also affect the kinds of samples that can be drawn and, consequently, the research questions may be constrained.[4] That is, it may not be possible to assemble one's subjects together so that group questionnaires can be used. It may also be impossible to use telephone methods because certain survey populations do not have phones or their phone numbers may be unavailable to the researcher. Mail-back questionnaires are limited because they often have such poor response rates that they are susceptible to nonresponse bias.

In addition to these defects is the problem that the major advantage of these methods—the anonymity afforded the respondent—can be a fatal disadvantage in two respects. First, because the data are given anonymously, the validity of responses is nearly impossible to determine. Second, longitudinal research, which has become an increasingly important method in some fields, is not possible with these methods.

Although exceedingly rare, the opinions of survey respondents regarding their preferences in survey methods are important to the issues just discussed. Fortunately, some data bearing on this are available from a survey conducted on behalf of the National Academy of Sciences (NAS). The Academy formed a Panel on Privacy and Confidentiality as Factors in Survey Response (1979) which undertook an exploratory research study of the opinions and perceptions of respondents about surveys. The results show that survey respondents have identifiable concerns over and preference for certain survey methods.

Respondents' past experience indicated that response rates varied by the type of survey approach. A clear advantage was evident for personal interviews, which had a response rate of 74 percent, compared to 55 percent for mail and 46 percent for telephone surveys. When asked about why they had failed to respond to a prior survey, the answers again differed by survey approach. Mail questionnaires were not completed due to oversight or procrastination. For telephone surveys, respondents objected to the method and distrusted an interviewer they could not see. Dissatisfaction with personal interviews was evidently not the cause of nonresponse.

Not surprisingly, when respondents were asked their preference in survey method, face-to-face interviews predominated with 51 percent, compared to 30 percent for mail and 7 percent for telephone surveys. The major reasons given for preferring interviews were that they are more personal, one can get help from the interviewer in understanding or answering questions, and one can trust them more (NAS, 1979: Table 34).

For several reasons respondents seem to favor the interview approach and are more likely to respond to this method compared to the more anonymous and impersonal approaches. Coupled with the fact that interviews do not limit the research process to certain kinds of samples, to certain kinds of designs, or to simple questions, there is an obvious need to develop procedures for protecting respondents in personal interview settings, rather than to seek alternate data-gathering methods that seem to be disfavored by respondents.

ADMINISTRATIVE STRATEGIES

One way to approach the problem of confidentiality in personal interviews is through administrative procedures which simulate anonymity following data collection. These procedures involve schemes for removing personal identifiers while maintaining the ability to link multiple data sources or follow-up interviews. A researcher may maintain two separate files: the data file with the names replaced by identification codes, and a file that links these codes with the corresponding names or personal identifiers. This will protect against many routine violations of confidentiality such as theft or unauthorized access to completed instruments. However, unless protected by statute, executive privilege, or other legal means, this method does not prevent the data from forced disclosure, as in subpoena. To avoid this, a researcher may contract with a third party—a so-called broker or custodian—to hold the linkage file. Such an agent should be able to resist government interference (e.g., by virtue of foreign residence) and, as part of the contract, agree not to return the linkage file to the researcher.

These administrative strategies may be fine in maintaining the confidentiality of survey data. At the time of the interview, however, respondents may not be aware of or may not appreciate the protection granted postinterview. It is easy to forget that interviews involve human subjects, subjects who are often distrustful of research and see little personal benefit in revealing the type of information being solicited. Indeed, one of the findings of the Panel on Privacy (1979: 123) should be considered in future efforts to survey sensitive topics: "One of the most striking features of these discussions was the nearly unanimous opinion of the participants that anything they said as respondents in surveys would not be kept confidential."

Clearly, some respondents will misrepresent their true status in sensitive surveys regardless of how strong the promise that their answers will be kept private. An acknowledgment that respondent cooperation and comfort, rather than suspicion and anxiety, may reduce response distortion argues for the application of techniques that the respondent perceives to be unconditionally effective in ensuring privacy.

NEED FOR AN ALTERNATIVE STRATEGY

There is one final limitation to all of the approaches discussed so far. Specifically, in many surveys it may be possible to determine the identity of at least some respondents on the basis of a series of answers. Even after removing or destroying identifiers, multiway cross-classifications of demographic data may produce some cells into which only one respondent can fit, thus destroying anonymity. To avoid this possibility, the researcher could be compelled to deal only with aggregate data, which would limit the analysis.

A data-collection approach is needed that:

(1) unlike anonymous questionnaires, allows the researcher to link together multiple waves of panel data or multiple data sources;

(2) unlike telephone or mail surveys, encourages participation through personal contact with an interviewer;

(3) unlike traditional interviews, does not provoke a respondent to conceal information that would be embarrassing to report in the presence of a stranger/interviewer;

(4) unlike standard confidentiality assurances, truly convinces respondents of privacy safeguards;

(5) unlike many administrative maneuvers to protect against threats to confidentiality, is absolutely immune to forced disclosures; and

(6) unlike all conventional approaches, does not permit respondent protections to be eroded through the discovery of identities from statistical analysis.

One such technique, known as randomized response, is the subject of this monograph.

2. THE RANDOMIZED RESPONSE TECHNIQUE

It may not be widely known that in a firing squad, not all the marksmen have live bullets. In Utah, for example, the only state that employs this form of capital punishment, one of the five sharpshooters, at random, is given a rifle loaded with a blank. The purpose is so that each can maintain that he had fired the blank, should his conscience force him to do so. Although it is possible to discern whether one has shot a real bullet or a blank on the basis of the rifle's recoil, it is not known until after the trigger is pulled. One can rationalize, therefore, that the act of pulling the trigger was not necessarily fatal.[5]

The same use of probability to assuage the conscience of members of a firing squad can be applied in social surveys of sensitive information. Since survey respondents tend to conceal embarrassing or threatening information, particularly when an interviewer (in person or on the phone) might disapprove, the element of chance can be used to inoculate their responses yet at the same time provide the researcher with sufficient data for analysis.

To illustrate hypothetically, suppose that one wished to estimate the prevalence of spouse abuse by surveying a gathering of men in an auditorium.[6] Of course, simply asking the men to raise their hands if they had beaten their spouse would most likely produce a roomful of rubbernecks but few raised hands. Instead, we could ask each of the men to flip a coin privately and to raise his hand either if he had abused his spouse or had gotten a head on the coin. Clearly, those raising their hands would hardly be implicated in abusive behavior, since most will be doing so because of obtaining a head on the coin flip. Even though we could not determine the true status of any of the hand-raisers, an estimate of abuse prevalence is available nonetheless.

Suppose that the room contains 100 men, 58 of whom had raised their hands. We can expect that half of the men would have received heads on their coins and thus raised their hands, regardless of their true status on the abuse question. The excess of eight hand-raisers would suggest that eight of the 50 who received a tail on the flip had in fact abused their spouses. Therefore, we could estimate the prevalence of wife abuse to be 8/50 or 16 percent, even though we could not determine which of the hand-raisers constitute the 16 percent estimated to have abused their wives.

Basic Randomized Response Strategies

The similarity between not knowing which of five sharpshooters in a firing squad are the four to have real bullets and which of the 58 hand-raisers are the 16 (the eight with tails plus a complementary eight with heads) who had abused their spouse should be clear to the reader. In practice, one might not attempt to survey large groups of respondents in convened settings like this. (If one could in fact gather one's sample together like this, in certain cases an anonymous questionnaire may be preferred.) Still, the same procedure and the same level of protection can be applied in a one-to-one setting.

This was the brainstorm of Stanley Warner—that the element of chance could inoculate responses to sensitive inquiries. His 1965 article, "Randomized Response: A Survey Technique for Eliminating Evasive Answer Bias," revolutionized the way that the sample survey could be designed. Though the crudeness of Warner's pioneering formulation limited the appeal of the randomized response method initially, many improvements and enhancements, which we shall review here, have significantly increased the value and acceptance of this approach. Warner's seminal approach may not eliminate evasive answer bias, as the title of his article boldly claims; however, it clearly points out a probabilistic logic to sensitive surveys useful for reducing response bias.

In a survey of abortion (particularly in the days when they were strictly illegal), a woman who had had an abortion might falsely deny the statement, "I have had an abortion," or, conversely, falsely affirm the statement, "I have never had an abortion." That is, it is not necessarily the true or false answer that is stigmatizing but the connection between the question and the response. Warner's suggestion was that a respondent be posed both questions but that she respond to one or the other depending on the outcome of a randomizing device (die, spinner, etc.) that only she sees. The response is no longer revealing, since no one except the respondent is aware of the question.

More formally, Warner's strategy directs the respondent to answer to one of the two logical opposites, depending on the outcome of a randomizing device, following a bernoulli distribution with parameter p:

> Question 1: I am a member of A.

> Question 2: I am not a member of A.

Elementary probability theory dictates that the total (regardless of question) proportion of affirmative responses, λ, can be expressed in terms of π, the probability of possessing the attribute in question (e.g., having had an abortion), in the following way:

$$P(\text{yes}) = P(\text{Question1})P(\text{yes}|\text{Question1}) + P(\text{Question2})P(\text{yes}|\text{Question2})$$

or, more formally,

$$\lambda = p\pi + (1 - p)(1 - \pi)$$

Solving for an estimate of π in terms of known p and $\hat{\lambda}$, the observed sample proportion answering "yes,"

$$\hat{\pi} = (\hat{\lambda} + p - 1)/(2p - 1) \quad (p \neq .5) \qquad [1]$$

having a sampling variance

$$\text{Var}(\hat{\pi}) = [\pi(1 - \pi)/n] + [p(1 - p)/n(2p - 1)^2] \qquad [2]$$

To illustrate, the IIT Research Institute (1971) surveyed the prevalence of various activities associated with organized crime in Illinois using the Warner technique. Each respondent was instructed to draw at random from a container of ten marbles, two of which were blue and eight of which were green (p = .2), and then to answer affirmatively or negatively to the appropriate statement:

> Blue: I have used heroin.

> Green: I have never used heroin.

This approach was repeated for a range of illegal activities, mainly involving gambling.

Despite the innovation, Warner's method had two severe limitations. First, as can be seen from equation 2, the variance of the estimator is considerably inflated over asking the respondent the sensitive question directly. Specifically, the first term of the equation is the usual variance of a sample proportion, and the second term therefore represents the additional sampling error due to the randomizing procedure. The closer the probability of selection, p, approaches .5 (and thus the more indeterminate the response), the greater the variance inflation. If, for example, a die is used with which the respondent is told to answer the first question if the roll shows 1 through 4, and the second question otherwise (i.e., p = 4/6), and if π = .20, the variance of the estimator will be inflated by over 15 times! Even a more modest choice of p of 5/6 triples the sampling variance. It is quite possible, particularly with a small sample size and a p close to .5, to operate under a $Var(\hat{\pi})$ that is so large that prevalence estimates greater than one or less than zero can result (see, for example, Reaser et al., 1975; Brown, 1975).

The second concern is less statistical in nature. Under this scheme, both questions deal with a very sensitive topic. Some respondents may wonder if there is some mathematical trick that will permit the interviewer to figure out what the status is. Even if the respondent appreciates the protection offered by the approach, the threatening nature of the topic itself may encourage a refusal to participate.

In an attempt to desensitize the use of an embarrassing question paired with its converse, Simmons (see Horvitz et al., 1967) proposed that the sensitive question be paired in a similar randomized scheme with an innocuous question. The so-called paired-alternative approach might present these questions:

Question 1: Have you ever had an abortion?

Question 2: Do you subscribe to *Newsweek*?

In this design, two parameters are unknown: π_x and π_y, the respective prevalences of abortion and of *Newsweek* subscribers. Employing (necessarily) two independent samples with different selection probabilities p_1 and p_2 ($p_1 \neq p_2$), the respective probabilities of affirmative responses in the two samples are given by:

$$\lambda_j = p_j\pi_x + (1 - p_j)\pi_y$$

for $j = 1,2$. The desired estimate of π_x, in terms of sample proportions of "yes" responses, $\hat{\lambda}_j$, becomes

$$\hat{\pi}_x = [\hat{\lambda}_1 (1 - p_2) - \hat{\lambda}_2 (1 - p_1)]/(p_1 - p_2) \qquad [3]$$

with variance

$$\begin{aligned} \text{Var}(\hat{\pi}_x) = &[1/(p_1 - p_2)^2] \\ &[\lambda_1 (1 - \lambda_1) (1 - p_2)^2/n_1 + \\ &\lambda_2 (1 - \lambda_2) (1 - p_1)^2/n_2] \end{aligned} \qquad [4]$$

One can greatly simplify the alternative question design and eliminate the need for splitting the sample by using an alternative response whose distribution is known in advance. For example, the question, "Were you born in November?" gives π_y of $30/365$. As a result, equations 3 and 4 reduce to

$$\hat{\pi}_x = [\hat{\lambda} - (1 - p)\pi_y]/p \qquad [5]$$

and

$$\text{Var}(\hat{\pi}_x) = \lambda(1 - \lambda)/np^2 \qquad [6]$$

Despite its obvious appeal, there may be practical limitations to using many of the demographic-type questions whose distributions would be known in advance. Incarcerated populations, for example, would rightly suspect their birth date to be known. Also, questions concerning birthplace might be given away by the respondent's dialect. Fox (1983) used mother's (or other close relative's) month of birth for a survey of weapons possession among high school students in Boston. Many respondents, particularly because of their age, may not have recalled their mother's birth month and may have made one up instead. Unfortunately, we do not really know what type of distribution these guesses would follow. That is, are there some months that come to mind quicker than others?

Additionally, there is reason to suspect that the birth month distribution may deviate from uniformity, particularly in certain regions of the country. Of course, one might opt for empirical estimates of the nonsensitive birth month distribution from site-specific vital statistics. However, many respondents (or their relatives in the above situation) may not be native to the site.

Though far more subtle, a survey by Bradburn and Sudman (1979) was flawed because of the overuse of birthday questions. In their survey, 12 questions were paired with different month-of-birth questions. That is, one question was paired with "Is your birthday in the month of January?"; another was paired with "Is your birthday in the month of February?"; and so on. It is likely that many respondents would have become suspicious after a few of these question pairs. Their suspicions would have been well placed. Since one can only give a "yes" response to one of the birthday questions, any respondent saying yes to more than one question pair would have been implicated in at least one undesirable behavior. The fact that the interviewer would not know which undesirable behavior might be sufficient protection for the legalist but would be of no consolation to the respondent.

Moors (1971) notes that, even when questions having known distributions are not available, the simplicity of the known π_y model can be achieved if one of the samples in the Simmons model were used exclusively to estimate an unknown π_y (i.e., $p_2 = 0$). In other words, a sensitive question is paired with a nonsensitive alternative in the first sample, and the nonsensitive question is asked directly in the second sample. Moors demonstrated that this modification could in fact produce a more efficient estimate of the desired π_x. Specifically, equations 3 and 4, by setting p_2 equal to 0, become:

$$\hat{\pi}_x = [\hat{\lambda}_1 - (1 - p_1)\hat{\pi}_y]/p_1 \qquad [7]$$

and

$$\mathrm{Var}(\hat{\pi}_x) = [\lambda_1 (1 - \lambda_1)/n_1 + \lambda_2 (1 - \lambda_2)(1 - p_1)^2/n_2]/p_1^2 \qquad [8]$$

Taking Moors's improvement one step further, Folsom et al. (1973) recognized that the two samples could be exploited far more efficiently by using two alternative questions, and not "wasting" one whole sample on just estimating the instrumental parameter π_y. As in Moors's plan, Folsom et al. (1973) suggested that the nonsensitive parameters be estimated directly. As in Simmons's model, both samples are still used for estimating the desired sensitive parameter. Specifically, in the first sample one of the nonsensitive questions is paired with the sensitive inquiry and the other nonsensitive question is posed directly. In the second sample the roles of the two nonsensitive questions are reversed.

For example, in the first sample respondents could be instructed to flip a coin and respond to a pair of questions as directed, and then answer an additional question outright:

HEAD: Did you cheat on your income taxes last year?

TAIL: Did you watch the 11:00 news last night?

DIRECT: Do you have any older living siblings?

Respondents in the other sample might be given the same procedure but with a different form of the interview schedule:

HEAD: Did you cheat on your income taxes last year?

TAIL: Do you have any older living siblings?

DIRECT: Did you watch the 11:00 news last night?

For the first sample,

$$\lambda_1^r = p\pi_x + (1-p)\pi_{y_1}$$

$$\lambda_1^d = \pi_{y_2}$$

and for the second sample

$$\lambda_2^r = p\pi_x + (1-p)\pi_{y_2}$$

$$\lambda_2^d = \pi_{y_1}$$

where λ_j^r is the probability of an affirmative response to the randomized response pair in the j-th sample; λ_j^d is the probability of an affirmative response to the direct question in the j-th sample; and p is the probability of selecting the sensitive question in both samples. Because, in essence, Moors's model is applied twice, two unbiased estimates derive from the sample proportions of affirmative responses:

$$\hat{\pi}_x(1) = [\hat{\lambda}_1^r - \hat{\lambda}_2^d(1-p)]/p$$

$$\hat{\pi}_x(2) = [\hat{\lambda}_2^r - \hat{\lambda}_1^d(1-p)]/p$$

[9]

having respective variances

$$\text{Var}[\hat{\pi}_x(1)] = (1/p^2)[\lambda_1^r(1 - \lambda_1^r)/n_1 + (1 - p)^2 \pi_{y_1}(1 - \pi_{y_1})/n_2]$$

$$\text{Var}[\hat{\pi}_x(2)] = (1/p^2)[\lambda_2^r(1 - \lambda_2^r)/n_2 + (1 - p)^2 \pi_{y_2}(1 - \pi_{y_2})/n_1]$$

[10]

A final estimate of π_x is given by a weighted average

$$\hat{\pi}_x = w\hat{\pi}_x(1) + (1 - w)\hat{\pi}_x(2)$$

[11]

where w is chosen to minimize the variance of the weighted average—which is achieved by setting w and $(1 - w)$ to be inversely proportional to $\text{Var}[\hat{\pi}_x(1)]$ and $\text{Var}[\hat{\pi}_x(2)]$. If the sample sizes are nearly equal, however, equal weights are usually sufficient.

Moors's design and Folsom's enhancement are both aimed at achieving estimates of the nonsensitive attribute to permit an estimate of the sensitive one. In actuality, it is not necessary to have a nonsensitive question at all, but to let the randomizing device itself generate the nonsensitive "responses." To illustrate the so-called forced-alternative approach, a respondent could be instructed to roll a die and to say "yes" if a one is rolled, "no" if a two or a three is obtained, and her actual response to the abortion question if a four, five, or six comes up on the die.[7] As a result, p = .5 and π_y = .33. Additionally, the hypothetical illustration given earlier in which men were told to raise their hands either if they got a head on the coin or had abused their spouses is a forced alternative design with p = .5 and π_y = 1.0.

Design Considerations in Randomized Response

Just as question wording and placement are critical features in the design of any survey instrument, there are also significant decisions that come into play in applying randomized response procedures. Insufficient attention given to choice of randomizing device and choice of nonsensitive questions (both their distributions and content) can doom a survey effort. Beyond the decision to use one sample or two, a known or unknown alternative distribution, a real nonsensitive question or responses generated or forced by the procedure, important considerations in choosing a randomizing device can greatly determine the level of respondent cooperation.

RANDOMIZING PROCEDURE

The choice of the value of p, the probability of selection for the sensitive question, involves the relative need for respondent protection and for efficiency in estimation. To afford greater protection for those asked to report sensitive information, the value of p should be as small as possible. The respondent will feel more comfortable if the chance of getting the sensitive question, or, more important, of looking like one is "probably" answering the sensitive question, is small. If the focus of the survey is very embarrassing or incriminating, one might select a value of .5 or even smaller. One of the advantages of a .5 selection probability, particularly when using unsophisticated or skeptical populations, is that many people wrongly believe that .5 is random and that anything else is "stacked." To cater to this misconception (even if it exists only at a "gut" level), a coin might be advisable.

The smaller the value of p (the fewer respondents who provide information relevant to the sensitive behavior), the greater the sampling variance of the estimator. Looking at equation 6, for example, a p of .5 inflates the variance of the estimate by four times that which would arise in a direct inquiry, whereas a p of .7 inflates it by only a factor of two. That the latter requires only half as large a sample as the former to achieve the same level of efficiency would suggest the following assertion: Make p as large as you dare (see Lanke, 1975). This is particularly true for small samples, when the level of sampling error is high. However, if one does anticipate a large sample, then a large portion of this wealth should be spent designing a procedure that will enhance the validity of the results.

Folsom (1974) attempted a randomized response inquiry of DUI (driving under the influence) arrests with a design poorly suited to protect respondents reporting arrests, and he paid for it in the quality of the responses. The unsatisfactory performance of the randomized response instrument in eliciting admissions of DUI arrests encouraged Folsom to reconsider. He admitted that "too much emphasis may have been placed on improving the precision of the method at the expense of its credibility" (Folsom, 1974: 53). He further recommended "moves to deoptimize the [randomizing] device like setting p, the probability of selecting the sensitive question, to one-half [which could] significantly increase cooperation" (1974: 54).

Essentially, the question is one of mean square error—that is, bias versus efficiency. In a small sample an unreliable estimate is of little value, regardless of the level of cooperation. But in a larger sample, once the level of sampling error is within reasonable bounds, more attention to reduction in response bias is appropriate. Unfortunately, no rule of thumb can be given for how large a sample must be before randomized response procedures with a comfortable level of p can be considered. It depends, of course, on the level of sensitivity of the inquiry among other features in the interview design. However, in one investigation of arrest histories, Tracy and Fox (1981) found that in terms of a mean square error criterion, a randomized response procedure with a p value of .5 outperformed a direct inquiry for any sample of more than 100 respondents.

The variance inflation produced by randomized response increases directly with the value of p. However, the reduction in response bias due to the sensitivity of the inquiry surrounds the extent to which the respondent feels protected by the design. While the statistician might realize that any value of p that is less than 1.0 in theory inoculates the responses, this would, of course, be insufficient for most nontechnical respondents. The degree of cooperation and truth-telling of the average respondent will depend on his or her subjective assessment of the degree of protection—on the perceived rather than the actual value of p. If, for example, a coin—unbeknownst to the respondent—were weighted to give 80 percent heads, the sampling error would be a function of .8, while the level of cooperation would be a function of a .5 p value. The researcher would have his cake and eat it too! Of course, this would be highly unethical, since there is an implied obligation to use fair coins. Nonetheless, the point remains that any randomizing device which is perceived to have a lower value of p than it really has will be desirable.

Moriarty and Wiseman (1976) conducted a small experiment in which they asked respondents to guess the likelihood of rolling a four through ten on two dice; of drawing a blue chip from a box containing one white, one red, and ten blue chips; of landing in a portion of a spinner that in actuality measured 7/8 the area of the circle; and of picking three cards from a full deck, without replacement, that were not all the same color. They found that on the average (median), the respondents guessed the probability of a four through ten on the sum of two dice to be .70, far less than its actual (.833) value. Apparently, people view the distribution of the sum of two dice to be much flatter than it is. Thus, using such a randomizing device would be desirable in terms of promoting cooperation while maximizing efficiency, without the ethical problems associated with outright deception.

In addition to the level of p produced by a randomizing device, the cost, feasibility, credibility, and performance of the device itself require careful consideration. Cards, coins, and dice are commonly used because, aside from their inexpensiveness and accessibility, respondents are familiar with them and therefore feel comfortable using them.

Naturally occurring random digits, such as the final digits on the respondent's social security number or those of the serial number on a dollar bill in the respondent's possession, have also been used in field studies. However, certain potential problems in accessibility and credibility arise. With certain samples, for instance, some respondents may not know their social security numbers offhand or may not have a dollar bill with them. In addition, some may question the randomness of these digits.

A number of investigators, such as Folsom (1974), have constructed elaborate randomizing devices and strategies which, despite their methodological elegance, entail procedures that are difficult to explain to respondents and thus make it difficult to convince respondents of their protection. Moreover, not all randomizing devices function well. Stem and Steinhorst (1984), for example, developed a multipurposed, forced alternative spinner that generated binomial, Likert, and poisson responses (see Figure 2). However, when shipped through the mail (for which it was intended), the spinner can get bent or otherwise damaged so that it no longer spins properly.

Reaser et al. (1975) designed a "cheap" alternative to the fifteen-cent die which they call a "random number target" (see Figure 3). The respondent is instructed to cover his or her eyes and to place a random mark with the point of a pencil on the target containing uniformly distributed digits from one to six, and then to answer the appropriate question corresponding to the number chosen. Indeed, a die may be bulky to mail and would usually be irretrievable, thus making the random number target economical for large mail surveys. Reaser et al. (1975) also claim (curiously) its superiority over a die in producing a uniform distribution, and thus suggest the use of a target in personal surveys as well. There is, however, a nontrivial probability of hitting a borderline—or at least of a respondent thinking that he or she had, thereby encouraging the respondent to impose a personal decision of whether to respond as directed by a digit or to repeat the process. Potential biases of this sort should be avoided at all costs.

Interestingly, it is possible to fashion a randomized response inquiry without using any randomizing procedure whatsoever (see Fox and

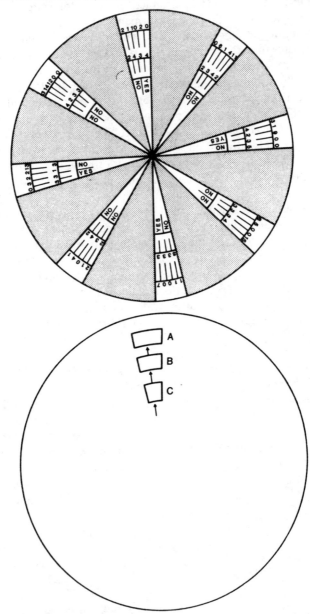

Figure 2: A Forced Alternative Spinner

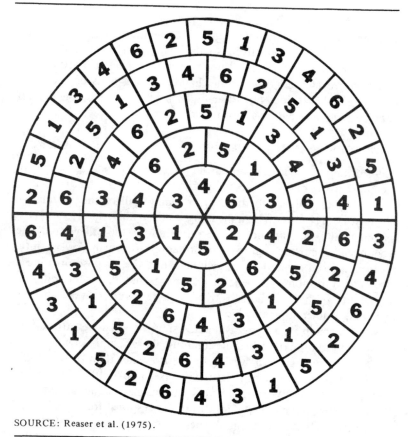

SOURCE: Reaser et al. (1975).

Figure 3: Random Number Target

Tracy, 1986). Relying on the addition rule of probability, one could, for instance, ask respondents to say "yes" either if they had had an abortion or were born in November. Because of the independence of the two items (which might be debated by those who are astrologically minded), the probability of a "yes" response would be

$$P(yes) = P(Abortion) + P(Nov) - P(Abortion)P(Nov)$$

Clearly, the prevalence of abortion can be estimated using the sample proportion of "yes" responses and the (approximately) known probability of a November birth month.

Apparently, avoiding the use of a randomizing device entirely does not remove the persistent dilemma of cooperation versus efficiency. Were one to use a nonsensitive question having a large probability (near 1.0), it would be extremely difficult to obtain a reliable estimate of abortion prevalence. On the other hand, a small, nonsensitive probability (like 1/12) does not offer much protection or ambiguity for someone who has had an abortion.

CHOICE OF NONSENSITIVE QUESTION

Returning to the usual randomized form of responding, the role of the nonsensitive question is equally critical. In the extreme case, where $\pi_y = 0$ (which reduces to direct questioning), all of the affirmative responses will be clear in their meaning. Additionally, the closer π_y is to 0, the smaller the variance of the estimate. On the other hand, the respondent reporting sensitive information is provided very little protection from a small π_y, largely defeating the purpose of using a randomized response. Whenever π_y approaches 0, the conditional probability of having the sensitive attribute given a "yes" answer, $P(A|Yes)$, is uncomfortably high.

More formally, a respondent possessing the sensitive attribute is jeopardized to the extent that the conditional probability of having the sensitive attribute given a "yes" response is greater than the unconditional probability of having that attribute (see Lanke, 1975; Leysieffer, 1975; Leysieffer and Warner, 1976). To minimize respondent jeopardy (i.e., to maximize the safety of an affirmative response for those having the sensitive attribute), p should be as small as can be efficiently afforded, and π_y should be large. Put simply, if a large proportion of the affirmative responses are to the nonsensitive question, then responding truthfully to the sensitive question will appear safe or nonjeopardizing for those who possess the sensitive attribute.

A corollary concern to protecting the respondent who in fact possesses the sensitive attribute is to avoid making the respondent not possessing the sensitive attribute appear as though he or she did. Clearly, a respondent not possessing the sensitive attribute should not be made to feel the need to violate the procedure by directly insisting on his or her innocence. A respondent making statements to the interviewer such as, "My answer is yes, but that's to the nonsensitive question," or "My answer is no, and that's to the sensitive question," should be avoided. Even worse, a respondent should not feel the need to deny the nonsensitive question when true just because he or she fears its implication concerning the sensitive attribute.

The "innocent" respondent will feel uneasy either if an affirmative answer is too misleading or if a negative answer is not sufficiently definitive. More formally, this respondent risks suspicion to the extent that the conditional probability of the sensitive attribute given a "no" answer is above zero.

To minimize risk of suspicion for the respondent not having the sensitive attribute, π_y should be as large as possible. Suppose, for example, that a substantial proportion of respondents are to answer the sensitive question (i.e., p of moderate size), and the nonsensitive question is, "Do you read two newspapers on a daily basis?" (i.e., $\pi_y \to 0$). Not only will the respondent who truthfully answers the sensitive question have little protection, but the respondent who does not have the sensitive attribute and answers the nonsensitive question in the affirmative is made to look to the interviewer very much as if he or she did. If, on the other hand, the prevalence of the sensitive attribute is similarly small, then the affirmative answer to the nonsensitive question will be less stigmatizing.[8]

Overall, the larger the values of p and π_x, the larger π_y must be to minimize respondent hazards (Lanke, 1975: 82; Greenberg et al., 1977: 54). It would appear, then, that a $\pi_y = 1$ is an obvious choice. That is (as in the early hypothetical illustration of a roomful of men surveyed about wife abuse), the alternative question is a directed response of "say yes." Not only is this affirmative response minimally risky for the innocent respondent and minimally jeopardizing for the respondent having the sensitive attribute, but a negative response definitely denies the sensitive trait.

Despite the apparent appeal of a π_y approaching unity, Greenberg et al. (1977: 57-59) note that this will produce less precise estimates of π_x. We tend to feel, however, that sacrificing precision for a reduction in response bias can be justified in most cases, except with exceptionally small samples.

One might wonder, in any case, whether with very small samples (say under 100) one can afford (in terms of loss in efficiency) to use a randomized response at all. We remind the reader that randomized response is an approach—one whose value depends greatly on how it is implemented. For such a small sample, one could use a high p value to provide protection in theory (which could be sufficient if an illegal behavior is under investigation). On the other hand, the small potential benefit from constructing a randomized response in this fashion may not warrant the time and effort it takes to explain to respondents a technique that seems strange to them.

RECONCILING RESPONDENT HAZARDS AND EFFICIENCY

It is easy to get confused in attempting to consider simultaneously the issues of respondent jeopardy, risk of suspicion, and sampling precision. Fortunately, each of these concepts can be quantified in order to reach optimal compromises.

Respondent jeopardy concerns the extent to which an affirmative response implies the sensitive attribute—that is, the conditional probability of the attribute given a yes response. For the alternative question case having a known distribution, we obtain (by applying Bayes's Rule)

$$P(A|Y) = \frac{p\pi_x + (1-p)\,\pi_x\pi_y}{p\pi_x + (1-p)\,\pi_y} \qquad [12]$$

These probabilities have been generated for 10 percent increments of p and π_y in Table 1, assuming, for the sake of illustration, a prevalence of the sensitive attribute, π_x, of 20 percent. Clearly, respondent jeopardy increases with increasing p and decreasing π_y. We might decide, arbitrarily, that any level of jeopardy greater than or equal to 50 percent is not tolerable—so that an affirmative response is probably not an admission of the sensitive attribute. Under this rule, any choice of p and π_y that lies above the dotted line in Table 1 could be termed allowable.

Risk of suspicion concerns, instead, the implication of a "no" response—that is, the extent to which a negative response still leaves the possibility that the respondent has the sensitive attribute. Again employing Bayes's Rule, the conditional probability of the sensitive attribute given a "no" answer, for the case an alternative question with known prevalence, becomes

$$P(A|N) = \frac{(1-p)\pi_x(1-\pi_y)}{p(1-\pi_x) + (1-p)\,\pi_y} \qquad [13]$$

Table 2 gives values of this probability for the same levels of p and π_y. Like respondent jeopardy, risk of suspicion increases with decreasing

TABLE 1
P(A|Yes) by p and π_y ($\pi_x = .20$)

p	π_y									
	.1	.2	.3	.4	.5	.6	.7	.8	.9	1.0
.1	0.345	0.280	0.255	0.242	0.234	0.229	0.225	0.222	0.219	0.217
.2	0.467	0.360	0.314	0.289	0.273	0.262	0.253	0.247	0.242	0.238
.3	0.569	0.440	0.378	0.341	0.317	0.300	0.287	0.277	0.270	0.263
.4	0.657	0.520	0.446	0.400	0.368	0.345	0.328	0.314	0.303	0.294
.5	0.733	0.600	0.520	0.467	0.429	0.400	0.378	0.360	0.345	0.333
.6	0.800	0.680	0.600	0.543	0.500	0.467	0.440	0.418	0.400	0.385
.7	0.859	0.760	0.687	0.631	0.586	0.550	0.520	0.495	0.473	0.455
.8	0.911	0.840	0.782	0.733	0.692	0.657	0.627	0.600	0.576	0.556
.9	0.958	0.920	0.886	0.855	0.826	0.800	0.776	0.754	0.733	0.714
1.0	1.000	1.000	1.000	1.000	1.000	1.000	1.000	1.000	1.000	1.000

π_y. Unlike respondent jeopardy, risk of suspicion decreases with increasing p, since the "no" response becomes more definitive. Setting, again arbitrarily, 5 percent as a maximum level of risk of suspicion, combinations of p and π_y below the dotted line in Table 2 are allowable.

Finally, the relative efficiency of a randomized response design is of importance, indeed critical, for smaller sample sizes. For the alternative question with known prevalence design, the sampling variance of the estimate is

$$\text{Var}(\hat{\pi}_x) = \lambda(1 - \lambda)/np^2$$

where

$$\lambda = p\pi_x + (1 - p)\pi_y$$

Dividing this into the variance of the conventional estimate, $\pi_x(1 - \pi_x)/n$, the relative efficiency of the alternative question with known prevalence design becomes

$$\frac{\pi_x(1 - \pi_x)p^2}{[p\pi_x + (1 - p)\pi_y][1 - p\pi_x - (1 - p)\pi_y]} \qquad [14]$$

Table 3 displays the relative efficiency of this randomized response plan for the same levels of p and π_y, revealing that relative efficiency (paralleling respondent jeopardy) increases directly with p and inversely with π_y. If we determine (again arbitrarily) that the relative efficiency must exceed 25 percent, those combinations below the dotted line in Table 3 are allowable.

Table 4 combines the information for Tables 1 through 3. For the criteria that $P(A|Y) < .50$; $P(A|N) < .05$; and relative efficiency $> .25$, three combinations of p and π_y provide allowable values, as indicated. We must emphasize that these results are specific to (1) the type of randomized response model employed, (2) the level of π_x assumed, and (3) the levels of jeopardy, risk of suspicion, and efficiency that are (subjectively) determined to be allowable.[9] Nevertheless, this example should reinforce the idea that the manner in which one implements randomized response may be as important an issue as whether one employs it at all.

TABLE 2

P(A | No) by p and π_y ($\pi_x = .20$)

p					π_y					
	.1	.2	.3	.4	.5	.6	.7	.8	.9	1.0
.1	0.182	0.180	0.177	0.174	0.170	0.164	0.154	0.138	0.106	0.000
.2	0.164	0.160	0.156	0.150	0.143	0.133	0.120	0.100	0.067	0.000
.3	0.145	0.140	0.134	0.127	0.119	0.108	0.093	0.074	0.045	0.000
.4	0.126	0.120	0.114	0.106	0.097	0.086	0.072	0.055	0.032	0.000
.5	0.106	0.100	0.093	0.086	0.077	0.067	0.055	0.040	0.022	0.000
.6	0.086	0.080	0.074	0.067	0.059	0.050	0.040	0.029	0.015	0.000
.7	0.065	0.060	0.055	0.049	0.042	0.035	0.028	0.019	0.010	0.000
.8	0.044	0.040	0.036	0.032	0.027	0.022	0.017	0.012	0.006	0.000
.9	0.022	0.020	0.018	0.015	0.013	0.011	0.008	0.005	0.003	0.000
1.0	0.000	0.000	0.000	0.000	0.000	0.000	0.000	0.000	0.000	0.000

TABLE 3
Efficiency by p and π_y ($\pi_x = .20$)

p	|				π_y					
	.1	.2	.3	.4	.5	.6	.7	.8	.9	1.0
.1	0.016	0.010	0.008	0.007	0.006	0.006	0.007	0.008	0.011	0.022
.2	0.061	0.040	0.032	0.028	0.026	0.026	0.027	0.029	0.035	0.048
.3	0.127	0.090	0.073	0.064	0.060	0.058	0.058	0.061	0.067	0.079
.4	0.213	0.160	0.133	0.118	0.109	0.104	0.102	0.104	0.109	0.118
.5	0.314	0.250	0.213	0.190	0.176	0.167	0.162	0.160	0.162	0.167
.6	0.429	0.360	0.316	0.286	0.265	0.250	0.240	0.234	0.231	0.231
.7	0.556	0.490	0.443	0.407	0.381	0.360	0.345	0.333	0.324	0.318
.8	0.694	0.640	0.597	0.561	0.532	0.508	0.488	0.471	0.456	0.444
.9	0.842	0.810	0.781	0.755	0.732	0.711	0.691	0.674	0.658	0.643
1.0	1.000	1.000	1.000	1.000	1.000	1.000	1.000	1.000	1.000	1.000

TABLE 4

$P(A|Yes)$, $P(A|No)$, and Efficiency by p and π_y ($\pi_x = .20$)

π_y

p	.1	.2	.3	.4	.5	.6	.7	.8	.9	1.0
.1	0.345	0.280	0.255	0.242	0.234	0.229	0.225	0.222	0.219	0.217
	0.182	0.180	0.177	0.174	0.170	0.164	0.154	0.138	0.106	0.000
	0.016	0.010	0.008	0.007	0.006	0.006	0.007	0.008	0.011	0.022
.2	0.467	0.360	0.314	0.289	0.273	0.262	0.253	0.247	0.242	0.238
	0.164	0.160	0.156	0.150	0.143	0.133	0.120	0.100	0.067	0.000
	0.061	0.040	0.032	0.028	0.026	0.026	0.027	0.029	0.035	0.048
.3	0.569	0.440	0.378	0.341	0.317	0.300	0.287	0.277	0.270	0.263
	0.145	0.140	0.134	0.127	0.119	0.108	0.093	0.074	0.045	0.000
	0.127	0.090	0.073	0.064	0.060	0.058	0.058	0.061	0.067	0.079
.4	0.657	0.520	0.446	0.400	0.368	0.345	0.328	0.314	0.303	0.294
	0.126	0.120	0.114	0.106	0.097	0.086	0.072	0.055	0.032	0.000
	0.213	0.160	0.133	0.118	0.109	0.104	0.102	0.104	0.109	0.118
.5	0.733	0.600	0.520	0.467	0.429	0.400	0.378	0.360	0.345	0.333
	0.106	0.100	0.093	0.086	0.077	0.067	0.055	0.040	0.022	0.000
	0.314	0.250	0.213	0.190	0.176	0.167	0.162	0.160	0.162	0.167
.6	0.800	0.680	0.600	0.543	0.500	0.467	0.440	0.418	0.400	0.385
	0.086	0.080	0.074	0.067	0.059	0.050	0.040	0.029	0.015	0.000
	0.429	0.360	0.316	0.286	0.265	0.250	0.240	0.234	0.231	0.231
.7	0.859	0.760	0.687	0.631	0.586	0.550	0.520	0.495	0.473	0.455
	0.065	0.060	0.055	0.049	0.042	0.035	0.028	0.019	0.010	0.000
	0.556	0.490	0.443	0.407	0.381	0.360	0.345	0.333	0.324	0.318
.8	0.911	0.840	0.782	0.733	0.692	0.657	0.627	0.600	0.576	0.556
	0.044	0.040	0.036	0.032	0.027	0.022	0.017	0.012	0.006	0.000
	0.694	0.640	0.597	0.561	0.532	0.508	0.488	0.471	0.456	0.444
.9	0.958	0.920	0.886	0.855	0.826	0.800	0.776	0.754	0.733	0.714
	0.022	0.020	0.018	0.015	0.013	0.011	0.008	0.005	0.003	0.000
	0.842	0.810	0.781	0.755	0.732	0.711	0.691	0.674	0.658	0.643
1.0	1.000	1.000	1.000	1.000	1.000	1.000	1.000	1.000	1.000	1.000
	0.000	0.000	0.000	0.000	0.000	0.000	0.000	0.000	0.000	0.000
	1.000	1.000	1.000	1.000	1.000	1.000	1.000	1.000	1.000	1.000

TYPES OF NONSENSITIVE ALTERNATIVES

An additional consideration in designing randomized response questions is the content of the alternatives. Obviously, it should address a nonstigmatizing characteristic to desensitize the focus of the inquiry. Also, it should not address a characteristic that is discernible, such as "Are you left-handed?" nor in any way reveal stigmatizing information about the respondent, as in Bradburn and Sudman's (1979) repeated use of birth month questions.

Though it may seem sterile and contrived to some respondents, the "forced alternative" approach has considerable appeal. First, because the "nonsensitive" parameter, π_y, is fixed by design, not only is the design simplified (since only one parameter needs to be estimated), but the sampling variance of the estimate of this parameter is reduced. Second, since the forced responses can be a part of the randomizing device itself, the administration of the method may be easier for respondents to comprehend, by not confusing them with two questions. Stem and Steinhorst (1984), for example, constructed a spinner having regions that are either preprinted with "yes" and "no" responses or else shaded, which would direct the respondent to answer the specified sensitive question (see Figure 2).

A final advantage of the forced alternative approach is that the investigator can set p and π_y to any values desired, so that the approach can be optimized in terms of respondent hazards and efficiency. For example, if, on the basis of Table 4, we desired a model with p = .7 and π_y = .8, we could use a spinner with 70 percent shading, 24 percent marked "yes," and 6 percent marked "no" (see Figure 4). Alternatively, although not exactly optimal, one could have a respondent roll two dice and respond as indicated below:

Roll 11 or 12: Say "no"

Roll 6 thru 10: Answer question "yes" or "no"

Roll 2 thru 5: Say "yes"

This would yield p = 23/36 = .64 and π_y = 10/13 = .77. Moreover, since respondent hazards (jeopardy and risk of suspicion) are a function of *perceived* p, whereas efficiency is a function of *actual* p, this plan might benefit from the tendency of respondents, reported by Moriarty and Wiseman (1976), to misperceive probabilities based on dice.

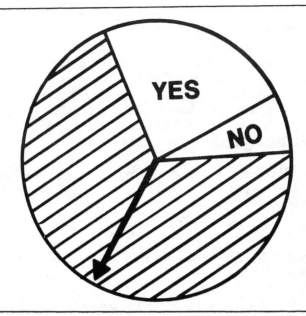

Figure 4: An Optimized Forced Alternative Randomizing Device

In a limited field test of the forced alternative method, Edgell et al. (1982) observed considerable resistance among respondents to saying "yes" when directed to do so, particularly when the sensitive behavior was having had a homosexual experience. Specifically, they used a microprocessor that would supply the random digits 0 through 9 on a screen. The digits 0 and 1 directed a "yes" response, while 8 and 9 directed a "no" response. The remaining digits directed the respondent to answer a particular question. Among a series of 55 randomized inquiries, 13 questions had "random" digits that were, unbeknownst to the respondents, preprogrammed to fixed values. Three of the set-up questions forced a "yes" response (i.e., a 0 or 1 would appear for all respondents). For these, 15 percent reported "no" to a tax cheating question, despite the "yes" direction; 11 percent refused to say "yes" when tied to a question of whether they favored the construction of a nuclear power plant nearby; and 26 percent said "no" although directed otherwise on a question concerning homosexual experiences. On four set-up items having a directed "no" in every case, nearly all the respondents complied.

The findings of this study are noteworthy, yet it was based on a small (n = 54) convenience sample of college students. Clearly, more research should focus on those conditions (e.g., type of sensitive question, or levels of p and π_y) which improve this form of randomized response.

Rather than a neutral question (e.g., birth month) or a forced alternative response, Zdep and Rhodes (1976) argue the benefits of using a socially desirable, nonsensitive attribute. For example, in a survey of child abuse using Folsom's two alternative question design, Zdep and Rhodes employed these questions:

Sensitive: Have you or your spouse ever *intentionally* used physical force on any of your children in an effort specifically meant to hurt or cause injury to that child?

Alternative 1: Have you attended church or synagogue within the past week?

Alternative 2: Have you attended a PTA meeting at school within the past 12 months?

The purpose is not just to desensitize the abuse response but to counterbalance it. That is, not only would a "yes" response not necessarily imply embarrassing behavior, but it might just as well imply socially desirable behavior.

Despite its initial appeal, this approach, unfortunately, can introduce considerable bias into the results. Zdep and Rhodes's survey, for example, seeks direct estimates of two nonsensitive prevalences to be used in estimating the prevalence of abuse within the randomized response pairs. However, under direct inquiry of a positive trait, a respondent may boast, which will inflate the $\hat{\pi}_y$ far beyond that operative when paired with the sensitive question. The overstated direct estimate of the nonsensitive parameters will in turn substantially bias downward the randomized response estimate of the sensitive parameter.

A socially desirable alternative question is designed to try to make the respondent feel as comfortable in giving a "yes" response as in giving a "no" response. Generally, the difficulty with the alternative question model is that it is not symmetric (see Bourke, 1974; Bourke and Dalenius, 1975); a "no" response definitively denies the sensitive trait (i.e., leaves no room for speculation), whereas a "yes" response can raise suspicion. In contrast, the original Warner design is symmetric; neither a "yes" nor a "no" answer is definitive in meaning.

An Alternative Strategy Using Sums

An extension of the randomized response method embodied in a new approach called the "item/count paired lists technique," developed by Miller (1984), avoids much of the confusion and distrust associated with the use of randomizing devices and of seemingly bizarre instructions for responding.[10] In this approach a respondent is given a list of behaviors, which includes the sensitive behavior of interest and a host of innocuous items, and is instructed to report *in total* how many of the activities in the list he or she has participated in. It is hoped that the respondent will feel comfortable reporting the total count, since this does not indicate in which particular activities he or she has been involved. Next, a second sample of respondents is given a similar list, but with the sensitive trait removed. Consequently, by subtracting the mean counts between the two samples, an estimate of the prevalence of the sensitive behavior is obtained.

Despite its apparent simplicity, the design considerations are complex. First, if the nonsensitive items are rare, any total count greater than zero will "look bad." At the other extreme, if the innocuous items are common, the total count could reach its maximum value, which would offer the respondent no protection at all. This would seem to suggest using (1) as many items as feasible and (2) items whose prevalences are midrange, so that the extremes are unlikely.

Difficult estimation problems arise, however, when using either a large number of items or ones whose prevalences are near one-half. The variance of the total count is composed of the variances of each of the items along with their covariances. If the sensitive item is low in prevalence, its variance, $\pi(1 - \pi)$, will also be small, particularly compared with the variance of the total count. Because the "true" variance of the sensitive attribute could be dwarfed by that of the total count, the reliability of the estimated prevalence of the sensitive characteristic is likely to suffer in the presence of the "noise" created by the other questions in the list.

Miller and Cisin (1984), for example, used the following two lists to estimate the prevalence of heroin use:

A	B
Rode in a car with a driver who "had too much to drink"	Rode in a car with a driver who "had too much to drink"

42

Placed a bet for $500	Placed a bet for $500
Tried heroin	
Parked illegally	Parked illegally
Tried to rescue a drowning person	Tried to rescue a drowning person

Estimates of heroin use were fairly imprecise because of its low prevalence in comparison to the totals. In some of the subgroup estimates, moreover, the heroin estimates were negative. Illogical results (and other logical but invalid estimates) can occur with this type of approach when, because of the greater sampling variability in the totals than in the sensitive item, the mean count for the second list exceeds the mean count for the first list, based on two independent samples of respondents. Nevertheless, because of its simplicity this approach does hold promise and therefore should improve with further refinements.

Generalization to Polychotomous Measures

The early theoretical and applied work in the area of randomized response was restricted mainly to the dichotomous case. Not only are the mathematics relatively simple, but the models are fairly easy for respondents to appreciate as well. Moreover, many of the types of application of interest solicit yes/no responses—for example, "Have you had an abortion?" "Have you been arrested for a DUI offense?" "Have you falsified your tax returns?" and "Did you vote in the 1984 presidential election?"

An obvious generalization of dichotomous randomized response models can be achieved by focusing on measuring sensitive attributes having several categories. Abul-Ela et al. (1967) demonstrated how Warner's approach to estimating a dichotomy with one sample (one degree of freedom is needed to estimate one parameter) can be extended to estimating a k-class multinomial. For this purpose, k-1 samples (and k-1 degrees of freedom) are required for estimating the complete distribution:

$$\pi_1, \pi_2, \pi_3, \ldots, \pi_{k-1};$$

and

$$\pi_k = 1 - \sum_{j=1}^{k-1} \pi_j \qquad [15]$$

For example, suppose that one seeks an estimate of a trichotomous distribution (i.e., π_j, j = 1,2,3). In each of two samples, respondents draw from a deck of cards alternatively labeled, "I am a member of Group A," "I am a member of Group B," and "I am a member of Group C." Let p_{ij} be the proportion of each of the three types of cards (j = 1,2,3) in the two samples (i = 1,2).

To illustrate, in a survey of sexual preference 12 cards might be labeled, "I consider myself heterosexual," 6 cards "I consider myself homosexual," and 2 cards "I consider myself bisexual" (p_1 = .6, p_2 = .3, p_3 = .1).

$\hat{\lambda}_1$ and $\hat{\lambda}_2$ are the observed proportion of affirmative responses in the two samples, and n_1 and n_2 are the respective sample sizes. After some extensive algebra, we find

$$\hat{\pi}_1 = [(\hat{\lambda}_1 - p_{13})(p_{22} - p_{23}) - (\hat{\lambda}_2 - p_{23})(p_{12} - p_{13})]/K$$

$$\hat{\pi}_2 = [(\hat{\lambda}_1 - p_{13})(p_{21} - p_{23}) - (\hat{\lambda}_2 - p_{23})(p_{11} - p_{13})]/K \qquad [16]$$

and

$$\hat{\pi}_3 = 1 - \hat{\pi}_2 - \hat{\pi}_3$$

where

$$K = (p_{11} - p_{13})(p_{22} - p_{23}) - (p_{12} - p_{13})(p_{21} - p_{23})$$

with variances

$$Var(\hat{\pi}_1) = [(p_{22} - p_{23})^2\lambda_1(1 - \lambda_1)/n_1 + (p_{12} - p_{13})^2\lambda_2(1 - \lambda_2)/n_2]/K^2$$

$$Var(\hat{\pi}_2) = [(p_{21} - p_{23})^2\lambda_1(1 - \lambda_1)/n_1 + (p_{11} - p_{13})^2\lambda_2(1 - \lambda_2)/n_2]/K^2 \qquad [17]$$

$$Var(\hat{\pi}_3) = [(p_{22} - p_{21})^2\lambda_1(1 - \lambda_1)/n_1 + (p_{12} - p_{11})^2\lambda_2(1 - \lambda_2)/n_2]/K^2$$

where K is defined as above.

As the number of categories in the polychotomy increases, so does the complexity of the estimation procedure. However, there has been some work in modifying and enhancing procedures for estimating polychotomies, although not nearly to the same degree as with dichotomies. Most notably, Bourke and Dalenius (1973) developed a general method for multiproportions that requires only one sample.

To estimate a trichotomy, for example, Bourke and Dalenius (1973) suggest using three types of cards, each type having all three mutually exclusive classes of the trichotomy presented, but in rotated order. Thus type 1 could list the statements in the order A, B, C; type 2 in the order B, C, A; and type 3 in the order C, A, B. The respondent would select one at random from a deck of these cards and then report the position number—first, second, or third—of the statement describing his or her status. The proportions (λ_i) expected to report each of the orders are

$$\lambda_1 = p_1\pi_A + p_2\pi_B + p_3\pi_C$$

$$\lambda_2 = p_1\pi_B + p_2\pi_C + p_3\pi_A \qquad [18]$$

$$\lambda_3 = p_1\pi_C + p_2\pi_A + p_3\pi_B$$

where p_j is the proportion of cards in the deck of type j $(p_1 \neq p_2 \neq p_3)$ and π_k is the proportion belonging to class k on the trait under investigation. Substituting sample proportions of respondents reporting order i for λ_i, one can solve for the desired estimates of π_1, π_2, and π_3. Finally, using a Latin Square type of rotation, this procedure can easily be generalized to any size multinomial.

Extension to Quantitative Measures

Of even greater practical significance than the extension to polychotomies was the generalization of the randomized response approach to quantitative variables by Greenberg et al. (1971), allowing the investigation of incidence rather than just prevalence. A survey of "How many abortions have you had?" may be superior in assessing the extent or rate of abortion than "Have you had an abortion?" because of the class of women who have had multiple abortions. Similarly, the recent interest in repeat victimization would require a quantitative model should one wish to employ randomized response.

Greenberg's model is a direct analogy of Simmons's two-sample, one alternative question model. Suppose that x is a numerical response to a sensitive question and y is a numerical response to some alternative nonsensitive question. Two independent samples of size n_1 and n_2 are employed, each with selection probability p_j $(p_1 \neq p_2)$.

For example, to estimate the incidence of assault victimization, we might have one sample answer one of the following questions depending on whether a die comes up 1 or 2 versus 3 through 6, and the other sample depending on a coin flip:

Sensitive: How many times in the past 6 months have you been assaulted?

Nonsensitive: How many weekly magazines do you subscribe to?

The mathematics are also directly analogous to the dichotomous case. Denote the verbal response given by the respondent (regardless of the question) as z. For the j-th sample (j = 1,2),

$$\mu_{z_j} = p_j\mu_x + (1 - p_j)\mu_y$$

where μ_x and μ_y are the means of the sensitive and nonsensitive questions, respectively.

Solving for μ_x, and substituting sample means for μ_{z_j}, the desired estimate of the sensitive mean parameter is

$$\hat{\mu}_x = [(1 - p_2)\bar{z}_1 - (1 - p_1)\bar{z}_2]/(p_1 - p_2) \qquad [19]$$

with variance

$$\text{Var}(\hat{\mu}_x) = [(1 - p_2)^2\text{Var}(\bar{z}_1) - (1 - p_1)^2\text{Var}(\bar{z}_2)]/(p_1 - p_2)^2 \qquad [20]$$

Though $\text{Var}(\bar{z}_j)$ can be estimated directly from sample responses, its value comes from a mixture of the distributions of x and y:

$$\text{Var}(\bar{z}_j) = [\sigma_y^2 + p_j(\sigma_x^2 - \sigma_y^2) + p_j(1 - p_j)(\mu_x - \mu_y)^2]/n_j \qquad [21]$$

As in the dichotomous case, the procedure is simplified if the distribution of the y question is known in advance. Only one sample is required, and equations 19 and 20 simplify to

$$\hat{\mu}_x = [\bar{z} - (1 - p)\mu_y]/p \qquad [22]$$

and

$$\text{Var}(\hat{\mu}_x) = \text{Var}(\bar{z})/p^2 = \sigma_z^2/np^2 \qquad [23]$$

As in the dicohotomous case, the choice of a value of p will depend on the relative requirements for efficiency and respondent cooperation. More important, however, is to try to ensure that the distributions of x and y are similar. Here the requirements for respondent comfort and statistical efficiency both point to maintaining a closeness of μ_x and μ_y. In terms of statistical properties, if the magnitudes of x and y differ considerably, the quality of the estimate of μ_x will depend greatly on how reliable the randomizing device is. Otherwise, the mixture of the two distributions in equation 21 will not be representative. More important, the distributions should be as similar as possible so that a respondent's answer will not indicate (correctly or incorrectly) from which distribution the response came. For example, if the sensitive question tends to elicit small numerical responses (e.g., "How many times have you been assaulted?") and the alternative elicited large numerical responses ("How many years have you lived in this home?"), the verbal response might give away the question.

Because, unlike the case of dichotomies, quantitative responses are usually unbounded, matching distributions (even in ranges) can be difficult. Thus the use of "forced responses"—having the randomizing device provide the alternative responses—becomes even more useful. For example, the spinner used by Stem and Steinhorst (1984), its functional problems notwithstanding, can be tailored to provide a nonsensitive distribution having the desired properties. The one they employed in their telephone survey, for example, had a poisson distribution with a mean of 3.60.

A forced alternative device proposed by Liu and Chow (1976), although expensive to construct, was adopted by Tracy and Fox (1981) in their methodological study of arrest frequency in Philadelphia. Fifty wooden balls were sealed in a lucite container having a neck large enough to house one ball (see Figure 5). Half the balls were red and half were plain-colored. Each of the plain-colored balls had a number painted on it from a known distribution (i.e., six with 0, seven with 1, four with 2, two each with 3 and 4, and one each with 5, 6, 7, and 8; overall, $\mu_y = 2.20$ and $\sigma_y^2 = 5.04$). The respondent would tip the device until a ball rested in the neck. If a red ball appeared, the sensitive question (frequency of arrest) was to be answered, but if a plain-colored ball appeared, he or she was to read the number off the ball.

An estimate of the mean of the arrest question is given immediately by equation 22, since μ_y is known. A further advantage of the forced alternative method is that, because the entire distribution of the

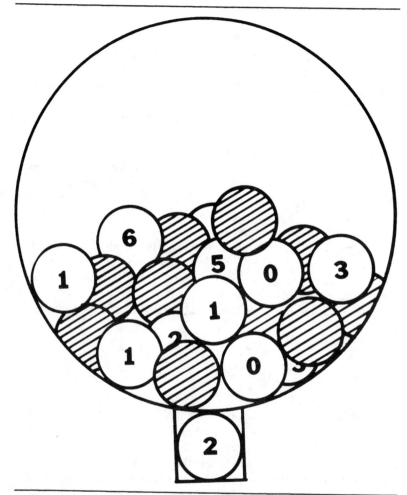

Figure 5: A Quantitative Forced Alternative Randomizing Device

alternative responses is known, one can estimate a complete frequency distribution for the sensitive question by repeated application of the dichotomous formula in equation 5.

Specifically, let $\hat{\lambda}_i$ be the proportion of respondents giving the value i, w_i the number of plain-colored (white) balls imprinted with the number i, and r and w the total number of red and white balls, respectively. The proportion of respondents with the value of i on the sensitive behavior is estimated to be

$$\hat{\pi}_i = [(r + w)\hat{\lambda}_i - w_i]/r \qquad [24]$$

The logic is straightforward. Using the distributions of Tracy and Fox, out of every 50 respondents, six 0s, seven 1s, and so on can be expected to come from the numbered balls. Therefore, for every 50 respondents in the sample, this distribution of responses can be removed, leaving behind an estimated distribution for the sensitive responses.

Just as Miller's item/count paired lists procedure avoided the use of a randomizing device altogether for measuring prevalence, so quantitative responses can be protected by using sums. Among a number of variations on the idea of using aggregate responses (e.g., Warner, 1971; Raghavarao and Federer, 1979), Himmelfarb and Edgell (1980) developed the "additive constants" approach. The interviewer instructs a respondent to add his or her sensitive score X to a random digit Y (from, say, a deck of cards) and to report the sum, Z = X + Y. The mean verbal response is known to be the sum of the mean sensitive response and the mean of the generated constants, as is true for the variances as well. Thus the mean and variance of the sensitive behavior is estimated simply by

$$\hat{\mu}_x = \overline{z} - \mu_y \qquad [25]$$

$$\hat{\sigma}_x^2 = s_z^2 - \sigma_y^2 \qquad [26]$$

The simplicity of this approach (assuming that respondents do not have difficulties in addition) may be outweighed by the significant problems in assuring protection for the respondent. First, unless the random digits have a range at least as great as that of the sensitive response, extremely large sums (X + Y) will implicate the respondent. In fact, any time the response exceeds the maximum constant, the respondent will have revealed a nonzero level on the sensitive variable. In certain applications, even this is too revealing.

Subgroup Comparisons

Our discussion thus far has focused exclusively on the development of prevalence estimates (in the cases of qualitative measures) and incidence estimates (in the case of quantitative measures) for sensitive variables, attempting to purge them of the effects of respondent falsification. Of course, the objective of most social science research goes beyond this descriptive posture, seeking correlates of attributes or behavior. We may not be as interested, for example, in the incidence of self-reported criminality as we are in comparing it across racial groups. Here the issues of response bias become more complex.

Respondent underreporting (or overreporting) of sensitive information, which can seriously distort univariate measures, has a different effect on comparative measures. For example, if all respondents tended to underreport their involvement in illegal activity by 50 percent, comparative analyses would be unaffected. If, however, different groups have varying propensities toward falsification, no comparisons can be made meaningfully. If one observes, for example, that blacks self-report more involvement in crime, is it an actual difference or just a reflection of a greater willingness to reveal the information? It is in reducing this type of systematic response bias that randomized response may be of the greatest value compared with direct questioning. To the extent that certain subgroups are more concerned about making a good impression on an interviewer (higher need for social approval), the results of direct surveys will be distorted. However, the desire to impress will be mitigated in randomized response inquiries, since the responses have little or no meaning in the eyes of the interviewer.

Technically, performing subgroup comparisons is quite simple. One can simply apply the formulas for estimating prevalence to separate partitions of the sample. Because of the greater inefficiency of randomized response, however, t-tests comparing groups means or z-tests comparing group proportions will be affected accordingly. That is, the power of the tests are blunted by the introduction of random error into randomized response measures and estimates. Nevertheless, testing for subgroup differences is surprisingly straightforward. Unlike the special formulas required to estimate rates, these tests do not require any modification of conventional formulas and statistical algorithms (see Boruch, 1971).

If the differences between the observed responses are significant, then the underlying estimated values are significantly different. Thus, if one wishes to test if the prevalence of spouse abuse varies between races, a chi square test can be applied to a 2×2 table of race by observed response (which may or may not concern abuse), assuming that the entire sample was interviewed in the same manner.

This might, at first blush, seem counterintuitive. Suppose that ρ is the true association between race and abuse. The observed association based on randomized response (say ϕ) will be attenuated because of the fact that only a portion of the responses are real and the rest are forced by design and thus uncorrelated with race. However, just as ϕ is smaller than ρ, so is the effective sample size reduced accordingly. Thus chi square ($= \phi^2 N_{effective}$; $= \rho^2 N_{actual}$) based on the observed randomized responses constitutes a valid test of the underlying association. Conversely, if $\rho = 0$, the observed responses should have the same distribution across subgroups (subject, of course, to sampling error). Hence, ϕ is also expected to be zero (and also subject to sampling error).[11]

To see this more clearly, consider the simple illustration in Table 5. The top panel provides a cross-tabulation of an attribute of interest (A/A') by two groups. The percentages having A (16 percent versus 28 percent) differ significantly ($\chi^2 = 9.0$). Rather than a direct survey, respondents are told to flip a coin and answer the question if a head appears, and to just say "yes" if a tail appears (i.e., p = .5; $\pi_y = 1$). The distribution of "yes" responses should appear like those in the middle panel. These observed responses are no longer significant ($\chi^2 = 1.5$) because of the reduction in power produced by adopting a randomized response approach. The bottom panel gives the estimates based on randomized responding. The estimates of the π_j's are as they should be. Further, a z-test of their difference is performed using a pooled estimate of the variance of the difference in proportions:

$$\text{Var}(\hat{\pi}_1 - \hat{\pi}_2) = \lambda(1 - \lambda)[1/n_1 p^2 + 1/n_2 p^2] \qquad [27]$$

where the pooled estimate of λ,

$$\hat{\lambda}_p = (n_1 \hat{\lambda}_1 + n_2 \hat{\lambda}_2)/(n_1 + n_2)$$

Note that a z-test of the difference between randomized response estimates is equivalent to a chi square test of the unadjusted, observed responses (i.e., $\chi^2 = z^2$).

The interest in subgroup comparisons is not limited, of course, to categorical variables (i.e., proportions). One can estimate the mean of a sensitive attribute for different groups or subsamples by applying the estimation formulas for the subgroups separately. Moreover, a test of the difference between estimated means on the sensitive variable can be easily accomplished by testing the mean differences in the sample answers to the randomized response questions. That is, the hard way of testing for differences would entail estimating the mean and its standard

TABLE 5
Testing Group Differences in Prevalence

Breakdown in Actual Data

	A	A$'$	Total
Group 1	48 16%	252 84%	300 100%
Group 2	42 28%	108 72%	150 100%
	90	360	450

$$x^2 = 9.0, \ p < .001$$

Breakdown in Observed Responses

	Yes	No	
Group 1	174 58%	126 42%	300 100%
Group 2	96 64%	54 36%	150 100%
	270	180	450

$$x^2 = 1.5, \ n.s.$$

Analysis of Estimated Rates

	Group 1	Group 2
n	300	200
λ	.58	.64
$\hat{\pi}$	.16	.28
$\hat{\pi}_1 - \hat{\pi}_2$		$-.12$
Var $(\hat{\pi}_1 - \hat{\pi}_2)$		.0096
z-value		1.2247
(z-value)^2		1.5

error for each subgroup and then constructing a t-test (or F-test for several subgroups) based on these statistics. The more direct method involves simply testing for significance in the observed (Z) responses using conventional procedures. In the dichotomous case, a chi square test of the randomized responses was equivalent to testing the underlying distributions; the same is true for the quantitative cases. Of course, the power of the t- or F-test is diminished by the nature of the random error introduced by the randomized response procedure.

Measures of Association

Rather than just looking at a subgroup comparison of the prevalence of some sensitive attribute across certain subgroups, one might be interested in the joint distribution of two sensitive attributes, both measured through randomized response. A test of the association of the two is obtained by a test of the observed yes/no responses, as explained earlier. However, we might also want to know the percentage of a sample having both of the two attributes.

The proportion of respondents giving "yes" responses to both to two randomized response questions is

$$\lambda = p_1 p_2 \pi_{x_1 x_2} + p_1 (1-p_2) \pi_{x_1} \pi_{y_2} + \\ (1-p_1) p_2 \pi_{y_1} \pi_{x_2} + (1-p_1)(1-p_2) \pi_{y_1} \pi_{y_2} \qquad [28]$$

where π_{x_j} is the prevalence of the j-th sensitive attribute, π_{y_j} is the prevalence of the j-th nonsensitive attribute or forced response, p_j is the probability of selection for the j-th question, and $\pi_{x_1 x_2}$ is the joint probability or prevalence of the two sensitive attributes. The joint probability can then be estimated in terms of observed $\hat{\lambda}$, known π_{y_j}, and π_{x_j} estimated in the usual way from equation 5. Once the joint probability is estimated, all other joint probabilities and conditional probabilities follow immediately.

To illustrate, consider a survey of illicit drug use in the military. Suppose respondents are confronted with these two sets of questions:

Head: Have you used marijuana in the past month?
Tail: Were you born between April and December?

Head: Have you used cocaine in the past month?
Tail: Is the last digit in your social security number greater than 4?

Here $p_1 = p_2 = .5$; $\pi_{y_1} = .67$ and $\pi_{y_2} = .5$. Equation 5 gives an estimate of the percentage who use marijuana and the percentage who use cocaine, while equation 28 gives an estimate of the percentage who use both drugs. Given these, one can calculate estimates of the percentage who use neither drug or the percentage of marijuana users who also use cocaine.

This can be generalized to the interdependence of polychotomies as well as the joint distribution of three or more attributes. Chen (1978 and 1979), for example, offers a log-linear model to accommodate such a generalization, but the details are too complex for this review.

Admittedly, simple descriptive statistics (e.g., proportions, frequency distributions, or means) and their breakdown by subgroups are quite restrictive analytically. That a majority of the theoretical and applied work using randomized response is focused on rather rudimentary statistical measures hardly implies any intrinsic limitation to the method. Unfortunately, there has been considerable misunderstanding in this regard among applied researchers. Many believe that, since only aggregate measures are available with randomized response, only statistical techniques appropriate for aggregates are applicable. Conversely, it is held that since the responses of individuals are unavailable due to the protections built into the method, many powerful statistical techniques designed for individual-level data cannot be employed. A recent comment of Sudman and Bradburn (1982: 82) is far from atypical:

> By using this procedure, you can estimate the undesirable behavior of a group; and, at the same time, the respondent's anonymity is fully protected. With this method, however, you cannot relate individual characteristics of respondents to individual behavior. That is, standard regression procedures are not possible at the individual level. If you have a very large sample, group characteristics can be related to the estimates obtained from randomized response. For example, you could look at all the answers of young women and compare to all the answers of men and older age groups. On the whole, however, much information is lost when randomized response is used.

While it is true that individual-level scores are not known, they need not be in order to invoke individual-level analyses. On an intuitive level, each individual could be treated as a subsample of size 1 whose "mean" score can be estimated. Of course, this would constitute a highly unreliable collection of estimated data because of the random noise produced by the method of randomized response. Nevertheless, the exact nature of this unreliability is known and thus is quite tractable.

That is, each individual score can be viewed as a special case of measurement error, a case in which the distribution of the measurement error is known. Therefore, it is only necessary that the analyst perform whatever corrections are necessary to adjust for measurement error or random noise to permit a full range of analytic approaches, including correlation, regression, ANOVA and other linear models (for a superb treatment of multivariate randomized response methods, see Rosenberg, 1979).

It was noted earlier that a chi square test could be used to test for the association between two categorical randomized response measures without having to estimate the underlying (joint or marginal) distributions. In the quantitative case, by analogy, a correlation coefficient between two quantitative randomized response measures performs a test of the presence of dependence between the two underlying sensitive variables.

The size of the observed correlation will, however, be attenuated. Suppose, in the extreme case, the two underlying variables were perfectly associated. The mixture of random noise into the observed randomized reports will make the observed correlation substantially lower than 1. This contamination, as we suggested, can be viewed as a form of measurement error, one whose behavior is known completely. Therefore, it is possible to correct for this attenuation to achieve a consistent measure of the underlying association.

This can be seen easily with the additive constants approach (see Himmelfarb and Edgell, 1980). Each observed variable is the sum of a true score plus a random term whose expected value can be set at zero and whose variance is known:

$$Z_1 = X + U; \; E(Z_1) = E(X); \; VAR(Z_1) = VAR(X) + VAR(U)$$
$$Z_2 = Y + V; \; E(Z_2) = E(Y); \; VAR(Z_2) = VAR(Y) + VAR(V)$$

By design, $COV(XU) = COV(YV) = COV(UV) = 0$; as a result,

$$r_{xy} = r_{z_1 z_2} \sqrt{s_{z_1}^2 / (s_{z_1}^2 - s_u^2) + s_{z_2}^2 / (s_{z_2}^2 - s_v^2)} \qquad [29]$$

where $r_{z_1 z_2}$ is the sample correlation between the observed reports.

The popular unrelated question model can also yield consistent estimates of correlations, although not so directly. Fox and Tracy (1984) have demonstrated how the Greenberg unrelated question model with the distribution of the alternative responses known can be reformulated (with some degree of algebra) into a conventional measurement model in order to correct for attenuation.

Consider a survey with two quantitative randomized response pairs:

$$z_1 = \begin{array}{l} x_1 \text{ with prob } p_1 \\ y_1 \text{ with probability } 1 - p_1 \end{array}$$

$$z_2 = \begin{array}{l} x_2 \text{ with prob } p_2 \\ y_2 \text{ with probability } 1 - p_2 \end{array}$$

The correlation between z_1 and z_2 can then be corrected for the effects of randomized responding to derive an estimate of the correlation of the underlying variables, x_1 and x_2:

$$r_{x_1 x_2} = r_{z_1 z_2} \sqrt{(1 + s_{u_1}^2 / s_{x_1}^2)(1 + s_{u_2}^2 / s_{x_2}^2)} \qquad [30]$$

where

$$s_{x_j}^2 = \left[s_{z_j}^2 - p_j(1 - p_j)(\hat{\mu}_{x_j} - \mu_{y_j})^2 - (1 - p_j)\sigma_{y_j}^2 \right] / p_j$$

and

$$s_{u_j}^2 = \frac{(1 - p_j)}{p_j} \left[s_{x_j}^2 + \sigma_{y_j}^2 / p_j + (\hat{\mu}_{x_j} - \mu_{y_j})^2 \right]$$

The extension to multivariate models can be accomplished in a couple of ways. First, one can construct a correlation matrix estimated as in 29 or 30 and use the matrix as input to a multivariate model. Alternatively, a LISREL approach can be fashioned in which a structural model of the underlying true variables $x_1, x_2, x_3, \ldots, x_m$ is joined with a measurement model of observed $z_1, z_2, z_3, \ldots, z_m$ and measurement errors $u_1, u_2, u_3, \ldots, u_m$ and their known variances.

The point that randomized response data can be given to elaborate analysis deserves emphasis, since the poor acceptance of randomized response in many applied circles may surround a misconception that randomized response is limited to univariate statistics. It is undeniable that the adjustments that may become necessary can be quite cumbersome. Nevertheless, there are many research areas—some of which are discussed in the next chapter—in which it is well worth the effort.

Disclosure Control

Although designed primarily as a data collection technique, the randomized response approach can be employed to inoculate previously collected data against the threat of forced disclosure by administrative or judicial investigations. Suppose, for example, a researcher has collected some sensitive or revealing responses in a direct inquiry survey and decides to guard against any threat to the privacy of the data. A certain percentage of sensitive yes/no responses could be altered or misclassified at random. Similarly, a certain percentage of the sensitive quantitative responses could be transformed by a random amount. In other words, the researcher could simulate randomized response after the fact.

Following these changes, the original data set would be destroyed, leaving the researcher only the transformed data. The new data could be analyzed using univariate and multivariate approaches as described above, or even merged with other data on the same individuals, since identifiers would still exist on the records. However, these data would no longer be of any use to those who would compromise the guarantee of confidentiality extended to respondents.

3. APPLICATIONS OF
RANDOMIZED RESPONSE METHODS

Since its introduction by Warner (1965), the randomized response method has been the focus of considerable theoretical literature. As Chapter 2 demonstrates, the original formulation by Warner has been exposed to continual revision and improvement. From a simple model to estimate the prevalence of sensitive attributes, the technique has evolved to the point where quantitative measures can be investigated and multivariate analyses can be applied.

Despite the strong interest of statisticians in reformulating the technique and expanding its research potential, the randomized response method has not been readily embraced by survey researchers. The quantity of literature reporting substantive applications of the technique is comparatively small in contrast to the theoretical literature. Most important, despite the fact that the prime value of the randomized response method is in its presumed ability to reduce response bias, applications concerned with validating the existence of this benefit have been exceedingly rare.

In this chapter we first review the substantive applications of the randomized response method. The reader should get the impression that these studies represent unrelated attempts to experiment with a novel and curious technique. With few exceptions, the application of randomized response has been more exploratory and methodological than substantive. We next discuss the studies which compared randomized response to other survey methods. Last, we present the results of the validation studies.

Substantive Applications

The earliest application of the randomized response method came just two years after the technique was introduced. Horvitz, Shah, and Simmons (1967) employed a two-sample, unrelated question design to estimate the proportion of illegitimate births among 148 North Carolina households. The sample was drawn so that all households had experienced a recent birth, and through the use of birth certificates it was also known that 18.9 percent of the households had had a birth recorded to an unmarried mother.[12] The randomizing device was a deck of 50 cards in which 35 had the sensitive statement, "There was a baby born in this household after January 1, 1965 to an unmarried woman who was living here," and 15 cards showed the nonsensitive alternative, "I was born in North Carolina." The proportions were reversed in the second sample.

The results were very similar between the randomized response estimate and the true proportion. An estimated 23 percent of the households reported an illegitimate birth, compared to the actual proportion (18.9%). The findings were even closer when separate estimates were computed by race. Whites reported 7.4 percent illegitimate births, compared to an actual proportion of 7.7 percent, while nonwhites reported 42.3 percent, compared to the true proporton of 45.4 percent.

The main conclusion offered by the researchers was that, given the incompleteness with which births known to be illegitimate are usually reported in household interviews, "the legitimacy status of births is sufficiently sensitive to warrant use of a technique which respects the privacy of the respondent" (Horvitz et al., 1967: 67).

Abernathy, Greenberg, and Horvitz have used the two-sample, unrelated question, randomized response design to investigate several public health issues in a large-scale survey in North Carolina. The randomizing device was a small, transparent, sealed plastic box which contained 50 colored balls, 35 red and 15 blue. The respondent was instructed to manipulate the box so that one of the balls would appear in a "window" visible to the respondent. Response to the sensitive question was keyed by the appearance of a red ball, while the alternative question ("I was born in the month of April") was cued by the blue balls. The samples consisted of nonoverlapping groups of women aged 18-44 (n = 1300) and women aged 18 or over (n = 1600).

Abernathy, Greenberg, and Horvitz (1970) reported the results concerning the prevalence of abortion estimated in the surveys. From the sample of women aged 18-44 it was learned that 3.4 percent had experienced an abortion during the past year. The prevalence was 1.3 percent for whites and 6.8 percent for nonwhites. From the second sample of women it was found that 4.1 percent had ever had an abortion, with nonwhites (10.2%) showing the higher prevalence compared to whites (1.6%).

The results were deemed significant in two major respects. First, it had been demonstrated that respondents would cooperate with randomized response inquiries compared to direct questioning. When asked directly if they believed that their friends would answer truthfully to direct questions on abortion, only 17 percent reported "yes." Second, the prevalence estimates obtained through randomized response, when converted to actual numbers of abortions, were seen as superior to the usual estimates that had disparate upper and lower bounds and thus were of little use for forming public policy.

In a related study Greenberg, Abernathy, and Horvitz (1970) reported survey results pertaining to other sensitive public health issues—the use of oral contraceptives and the existence of emotional problems which required professional help. For both issues, the researchers reported that the randomized response estimates were close enough to other reported findings to be credible and reliable.

Given the sensitivity of the issues investigated, from abortion to emotional problems, the authors were satisfied that the randomized response approach can provide answers to a number of sensitive questions in the field of public health which had been previously studied in only a limited fashion.

Liu and Chow (1976) field-tested a multiple trial randomized response technique in Taiwan. Three hundred women were surveyed using the unrelated question approach (with p = 0.3) to obtain estimates of induced abortion. Half of the sample were given one trial, while the other half were asked to respond three times. The goal was not only to obtain estimates of abortion but to determine if multiple trials would improve the efficiency of estimation. Liu and Chow reported that the three-trial estimate was higher than that obtained in a single trial (.303 versus .282). Both estimates were considerably higher than previous estimates obtained through direct question methods.

Shimizu and Bonham (1978) also applied randomized response to the topic of abortion. The respondents were a national multistage probability sample of women 15-44 years of age. The unrelated question design was used with two nonsensitive alternatives and a coin toss for question selection. Shimizu and Bonham found a much higher prevalence of abortion than had been found in previous direct surveys.

As part of a study of organized crime activities, the IIT Research Institute (1971) utilized the original Warner (1965) formulation of randomized response to estimate the proportion of 1200 Illinois households in which a person had engaged in various forms of gambling or had used heroin. The randomizing device consisted of a container of ten colored marbles, two of which were blue and posed a sensitive question, and eight of which were green and directed its converse. The results showed that organized crime activities, as evidenced by the prevalence of gambling and heroin use, were a significant problem in Illinois. The randomized response technique was considered successful because it achieved population estimates of these illegal activities which has proven to be elusive in previous research.

Dawes (1974) used a simple coin toss design to estimate the prevalence of several sensitive behaviors (drug use, cheating, stealing, sexual activity, and lying) among a sample of 270 college students. Geurts, Andrus, and Reinmuth (1975) adopted randomized response to study shoplifting and other deviant behavior in retail stores. They used a two-sample approach with two randomizing devices with different probability distributions. Madigan, Abernathy, Herrin, and Tan (1975) employed a randomized response approach to estimate the extent of purposive concealment of deaths in a household survey in the Philippines which was designed to measure population and vital events.

Comparison Studies

Several research efforts which utilized randomized response were conducted not to show that the technique could be applied successfully in the field, nor to obtain sample estimates of sensitive attributes, but rather to compare the method with more traditional means of collecting survey data. Although none of the studies utilized criterion measures for which the true values were known, and thus the studies cannot properly be called validation efforts, these research applications confronted directly the relative success with which different methods of survey questioning obtained estimates of sensitive behaviors.

The Human Resources Research Organization, through funding by the Department of the Army, conducted three studies to compare randomized response to other methods of collecting data on drug use among military personnel. The first study, by Brown and Harding (1973), attempted to measure the prevalence of drug use (marijuana, hallucinogens, amphetamines, barbiturates, and narcotics) among 1100 officers and enlisted men. Three data collection methods were used: a 62-item questionnaire, a card-sort technique, and a randomized response design. Adopting Simmons's unrelated question method, a deck of 50 cards was used, with 40 sensitive and 10 nonsensitive questions for the first half-sample and the reverse for the second half-sample.

The results for both enlisted men and officers showed that randomized response obtained higher estimates than did an anonymous questionnaire. The card-sort approach was viewed as totally unsuccessful in obtaining the required data. Among enlisted men, randomized response achieved higher estimates than the questionnaire for hallucinogens (21 percent versus 17 percent), amphetamines (18 percent versus 16 percent), barbiturates (17 percent versus 10 percent), and narcotics (6 percent versus 5 percent). Only in the case of marijuana use did the questionnaire (39 percent) obtain a higher prevalence than randomized response (36 percent).

Among the officers, whom the researchers speculated would feel more threatened concerning the consequences of admitting drug use, the randomized response method worked consistently better than the questionnaire and produced more disparate estimates. The prevalence obtained by randomized response versus questionnaire was 9.0 percent versus 5.0 percent for marijuana, 11.6 percent versus 1.6 percent for hallucinogens, 8.0 percent versus 1.9 percent for amphetamines, 7.9

percent versus 0.6 percent for barbiturates, and 4.0 percent versus 0.3 percent for narcotics.

In a second study Reaser, Hartsock, and Hoehn (1975) investigated the differences among conventional questionnaires and two randomized response designs. The researchers used a forced alternative randomized response procedure in which the respondent was directly either to answer the sensitive question honestly or to say "yes" (without an alternative nonsensitive question), depending on the outcome of the randomizing device. The device was a random number target which (see Figure 3), when used by the respondent, signaled him or her to answer the sensitive question or to give the "nonsensitive" yes response. The two randomized response conditions differed only in terms of the probability of having to answer the sensitive question. In one condition the probability was .5 (FARR-50), while in the other it was .83 (FARR-83). The sample consisted of 3000 company grade officers, and the survey was conducted through the mail.

The results indicated that the FARR-83 approach produced higher estimates of drug use, racial prejudice, and dissatisfaction with the army than did the traditional questionnaire. The FARR-50 method, which forced the respondent to say "yes" half of the time, did not perform as well as the FARR-83 or the conventional questionnaire.

The third project (Brown, 1975) involved a mail survey of 4000 junior officers and enlisted men regarding drug use (marijuana, psychedelics, stimulants, depressants, and narcotics) over the previous three days. A traditional questionnaire was compared to randomized response. The latter design was the unrelated question approach, which paired five different innocuous questions with the drug questions. The sets of innocuous questions were different for the officers and enlisted men. The randomizing process instructed the respondent to answer the sensitive question if his mother was not born in November.

The findings did not show significant differences by method. For both junior officers and enlisted men, conventional questionnaires and randomized response inquiries produced nearly equivalent drug use prevalence rates. Brown (1975: 27) concluded that if the randomized response approach is to have any advantage over conventional questionnaires in the conduct of mail surveys, "the subject must be able to see for himself that his selection of questions is determined by chance." Brown further noted that the probabilistic process must operate in the presence of the subject. He thus believed that because the randomizing procedure, month of mother's birth, operated independently of the respondent, the subject became suspicious and the technique's effectiveness was vitiated.

Goodstadt and Gruson (1975) also utilized randomized response to obtain drug use estimates. The sample was 854 Ontario high school students. The design was a two-group, two unrelated questions randomized response approach with the last digit of the subject's telephone number serving as the randomizing device. The probability of answering the sensitive question was .30.

The students were significantly more likely to respond to drug use questions under the randomized response condition than under traditional direct questioning. Estimates pertaining to the use of six drugs during the preceding three months were significantly higher for randomized response than for direct questions for five of the drugs, including alcohol, cannabis, amphetamines, tranquilizers, and heroin. Only in the case of hallucinogen use were the usage rates the same for each condition.

In addition to drug use surveys, researchers have taken a comparative approach in the study of abortion. I-Cheng et al. (1972) used a randomized response method in Taiwan for a sample of 692 women and a direct question sample of 1102 women. In all, 28 percent of the former, compared to 12.7 percent of the latter, admitted to at least one induced abortion.

Krotki and Fox (1974) compared randomized response to both questionnaires and interviews concerning recent and lifetime abortions, premarital sex, premarital pregnancy, illegitimate children, and contraceptive use in a sample of 1045 Edmonton women aged 18 to 54. The randomized response method was the unrelated question approach achieved through the use of a clear plastic box containing 50 balls, of which 35 were blue and keyed the sensitive question and 15 were red and directed the nonsensitive question.

The research indicated that randomized response estimates were higher than those obtained by anonymous questionnaires, which in turn were higher than those obtained from interviews. Although the prevalence rates were similar for the two most anonymous conditions, randomized response and mail-back questionnaires, randomized response elicited greater respondent cooperation, as 97 percent of the subjects in this condition completed the survey as opposed to 73 percent of those in the questionnaire condition. Thus randomized response was more successful because it facilitated both respondent cooperation and reporting.

In a study of self-reported delinquency among Seattle youth, Weis and Alstyne (1979) compared anonymous questionnaires, face-to-face interviews, and the unrelated question randomized response design. This research failed to find significant differences across the three data gathering conditions. Because differences favoring randomized response were expected, the researchers noted that several factors such as respondent age, overreporting in the other interview conditions, and the sensitivity of the behaviors may have operated to reduce the success of the randomized response technique.

Himmelfarb and Licksteig (1982) compared direct questions to randomized response for 56 desirable and undesirable attributes or behaviors. A third interview question was used to determine the desirability/undesirability of the items. Thus this research not only compared direct and randomized questions but also tried to explain or predict the difference in estimates by the perceived sensitivity of the items. Although the paper did not present tests of the randomized response versus direct question differences, the research did indicate that the observed differences were related to the sensitivity of the items. Generally, higher estimates of undesirable items were obtained under randomized response compared to direct questions.

Durham and Lichtenstein (1983) used a sample of college students to test the abilities of randomized response and anonymous questionnaires (administered in a group setting) to elicit responses concerning a range of criminal behaviors. The research attempted to derive estimates of both the prevalence and incidence of the sensitive behaviors. With respect to the prevalence estimates, the results were mixed. Five of the 19 items significantly favored randomized response, while three of the items significantly endorsed the group-administered questionnaires. The comparisons of means for the incidence data showed that significant differences were obtained for only two items, and these favored the questionnaire method. In discussing the results, the authors noted that three important criteria necessary to test randomized response were not present: a threat to anonymity, sensitivity of survey questions, and nonrare behaviors.

Validation Research

To date, there have been four substantial research efforts that have attempted to investigate, using a known criterion, whether randomized response does in fact produce response estimates of sensitive behaviors that are less distorted than estimates obtained through the more traditional survey methods. As noted earlier, the vast majority of previous applications have been either randomized response-only designs or comparative research, which, because it lacked data on the subjects' true status for the sensitive attribute, could not validate the reduction in error achieved through randomized response methods.

Folsom (1974) used a sample of persons who were known to have been arrested for driving under the influence (DUI). He compared a direct question condition, a self-administered questionnaire, to randomized response with two conditions which varied the probability of selecting the sensitive question. Like many randomized response studies, the randomizing device was a container that held 50 balls of different colors.

Folsom found that the randomized response procedure failed to perform better than the anonymous questionnaire in eliciting an admission of a DUI arrest. In all, 84 percent of the direct subjects admitted their arrest, compared to 72 percent of the respondents in the randomized response conditions.

One must consider, first, whether an anonymous questionnaire provides an appropriate standard of comparison for evaluating the relative quality of randomized responses. Few have challenged the superiority of anonymous instruments for soliciting sensitive information, but rather their analytic richness (see Chapter 1, p. 13). More appropriately, randomized response should be compared with other nonanonymous survey procedures.

According to Folsom himself, moreover, his study suffered from several problems that appeared to have affected the performance of randomized response (see Chapter 2, p. 25). The randomizing device produced very revealing response combinations. Because randomized response is intended to safeguard subjects by destigmatizing their answers, the Folsom respondents were sufficiently jeopardized so as to reduce the protection.

Locander, Sudman, and Bradburn (1976) compared sample estimates with the known proportions of respondents who recently had been charged with drunken driving, been involved in a bankruptcy, registered to vote, obtained a library card, or voted in a primary. In addition to varying the level of sensitivity or threat in the question, the research varied the level of anonymity by using face-to-face interviews, telephone interviews, self-administered questionnaires, and the unrelated question randomized response design.

Randomized response outperformed, although not significantly, the other methods in eliciting truthful responses to the sensitive questions. The results were encouraging but far from definitive. The sizes of the validation samples were extremely small. For example, true scores for the most sensitive question, DUI arrests, were available for just 23 respondents. Thus it is unlikely that differences would have been significant.

Lamb and Stem (1978) conducted a comparative validation study in which dichotomous and quantitative models were used. A convenience sample of college students was used to compare estimated versus actual behavior using a conventional interview and randomized response. The sensitive questions pertained to whether the respondent had failed a course and how many courses had been failed. The true scores for respondents were available from the school's registrar.

The results indicated that both randomized response and the traditional interview were effective in estimating the proportion of respondents who had previously failed a course. In both conditions the reported prevalence was not statistically different from the true proportion. However, with respect to the incidence of failing courses, randomized response produced better estimates. That is, under direct questioning respondents significantly underreported the number of times they had failed a course. Under randomized response the estimated incidence was lower, but not statistically different from the true value. The researchers concluded that randomized response showed promise for improved estimation in marketing studies of sensitive issues (Lamb and Stem, 1978: 621).

Tracy and Fox (1981) conducted a field-validation of a quantitative randomized response model. They compared self-reports of past criminal behavior (more exactly, arrests) obtained in a direct question condition with estimates obtained from randomized response. Because the respondents were sampled from criminal history records, true scores regarding the number of official arrests were available as a validation criterion. The randomizing device was a clear container with colored balls (see Figure 5) similar to the device used by Liu and Chow (1976). Tracy and Fox's research favored randomized response in several respects.

First, although response error—the underreporting of arrests—was evident for both randomized response and direct question, the former achieved a 15 percent reduction in error compared to the latter. Second, the error in the direct question condition was not only greater, it was significantly related to respondent characteristics, with 54 percent of such error being explained by characteristics such as sex, race-sex interaction, income, need for approval, and number of arrests. In contrast, although attenuated, only 1 percent of the error in randomized response was explained by respondent characteristics, none of which had significant coefficients. Third, when response error was partitioned, it was found that constant bias and especially systematic bias were much more substantial in the direct question condition than in randomized response.

4. CONCLUSION

Suppose that an economist was interested in conducting a two-wave panel study of self-reported taxpayer compliance in order to evaluate upcoming changes in the tax code. The panel nature of the design would rule out the use of anonymous procedures such as a self-administered questionnaire. The researcher must employ a data collection method that maintains respondent confidentiality but, at the same time, allows the responses from the same individuals, surveyed in consecutive years, to be linked. A model link-file system, developed for the American Council of Education's Office of Research, was conceived for precisely such a research need.

The so-called ACE system (Astin and Boruch, 1970) uses four files to accomplish a two-wave panel. This data management strategy, schematically illustrated in Figure 6, is best described by one of its developers:

The ACE system was developed in direct response to public and professional apprehension about maintaining identifiable records on respondents in longitudinal research on political activism among American college students. Under the model, identifiable data are collected by the researcher at stage 1 and then transformed into three files. One file consists of records that contain only statistical data (i.e., no identifiers), each record being coupled to an arbitrary account number (XI' in the diagram). A second file is created, containing true identifiers, each of which is coupled to a second arbitrary accounting number (II"). The third file is a code linkage, a file that matches the two sets of accounting numbers and therefore would permit total identifications of records if the three files were merged, shown as I' I" at stage 2 . . . This last file is

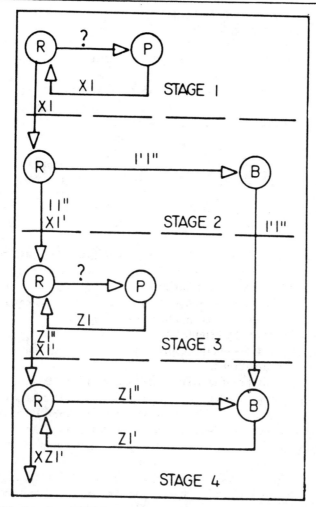

SOURCE: Boruch and Cecil (1979). Reprinted by permission of the authors.

Figure 6: The ACE System

maintained by a broker who is independent of the agency actually eliciting and maintaining the data. The broker is under contract not to disclose the code linkage system to anyone, including a government agency, for any reason. The ACE Office of Research code linkage, for example, was maintained by a social researcher in a foreign country in order to assure that research data concerning political activists on college campuses could not be appropriated for nonresearch use. Ideally, the broker is an agency that can legally resist both government interrogation and illegal attempts to acquire the file.

New identifiable data (ZI), collected from the sample at stage 3, are also transformed. True identifiers are replaced by the second set of arbitrary accounting numbers, yielding a file designated ZI''. This file of statistical records, each coupled to an accounting number, is shipped to the broker, who then substitutes the first accounting number set for the second set: each record ZI'' is changed to ZI'. Finally, the file is returned to ACE, where data from stage 1 and stage 3 can be linked using the accounting numbers common to both files (i.e., XI' is linked to ZI') as a basis for matching [Boruch and Cecil, 1979: 109-110].[13]

This approach leaves a number of questions: (1) Is ACE truly invulnerable to forced disclosure? (2) Does ACE prohibit the identification of certain respondents on the basis of their unique constellation of responses? (3) If the researcher ventures to explain the safeguards to the respondent, can it be accomplished in simple enough terms, and might it not backfire by heightening rather than dispelling respondent skepticism? and (4) Would the respondent believe the safeguards even if he or she understood them?

Instead of this link-file system, the economist could utilize randomized response to collect data on a topic as sensitive as taxpayer compliance. Not only could he or she obtain and compare estimates of compliance before and after the introduction of changes in the code, but it is possible to analyze the relationship between individual compliance and various demographic, socioeconomic, and attitudinal measures contained in the interview schedule without legally jeopardizing the respondents. Moreover, these data could even be linked and merged with official tax return data on reported income, deductions, and so on for further analysis, again without concern over IRS interference with respect to the self-reported compliance data.

Randomized response represents a promising alternative to other methods for both increasing respondent cooperation and safeguarding the privacy of responses. Not only is it "foolproof" in an ethical sense, but it is analytically superior to other anonymous procedures and apparently more protective in the eyes of respondents than various administrative schemes for maintaining confidentiality postinterview.

We do not suggest, however, that the randomized response approach is advisable in all survey situations. Many investigations are absolutely or relatively innocuous and nonthreatening to respondents and so randomized response would not be warranted. Yet other topics, which because of their sensitivity and threatening nature would ordinarily be difficult if not impossible to survey, are quite researchable with randomized response. Also, small-scale research can be problematic in terms of applying randomized response owing to its inefficiency relative to traditional direct inquiries. Yet only moderate samples are required before the potential reduction in systematic response bias possible with randomized response overtakes the drop in efficiency.

Prior to its implementation in large, expensive surveys, the investigator certainly should pilot test the randomized response procedure. The applied literature reveals numerous cases in which poor construction or administration has vitiated the potential for the technique. Although pretesting any survey instrument is, of course, always wise, this prescription is far more urgent with randomized inquiry because of its unfamiliarity to both respondents and interviewers alike.

It does seem that the randomized response approach has not been exploited to any great degree in the social sciences, particularly those areas of research in which the technique is best suited (e.g., studies of criminality). Randomized response affects the entire makeup of the research design, from the construction of data collection instruments, to interviewing techniques, to methods of analysis. Unlike other methodological advances in social statistics, the decision to use randomized response is irreversible. For example, if one were to try LISREL modeling on a particular data set and were dissatisfied, that would hardly prevent one from abandoning that approach and using something different, perhaps something more familiar. Randomized response, however, alters the data themselves. Therefore, the researcher must carefully consider this feature of research design from the earliest stages of the research process. Moreover, he or she needs to understand those limitations that are real and those that are just imagined.

Finally, our previous comments and our overall emphasis in this monograph may give the impression that randomized response fundamentally alters the conduct of the entire survey. Though this may have been true in some of the applications we reviewed, randomized response can be limited to as few as one question in a survey, thereby leaving unaffected the rest of the survey design and data collection effort. Fox (1983), for example, conducted half-hour interviews with 500 high school students in Boston, dealing with their attitudes toward school, peers, teachers, and administrators, their feelings of safeness or fear in and around school, and their personal victimization experiences. All of these areas were explored with face-to-face direct questioning.

Interviews were seen as the "only" viable method, since questionnaires would hardly achieve the same level of respondent cooperation, participation, and responsiveness or the same degree of detail. One question, however, dealt with the possession of a weapon at school. There was serious concern on the part of school administrators over the privacy of this information. Even if the interviews were stripped of identifiers, it would be possible on the basis of other information elicited in the survey to identify many of the students. Randomized response provided the mechanism for asking this one question rather than altering the entire nature of the research design to accommodate this one area of interest or dropping this item from the interview completely.

In sum, randomized response carries considerable potential in a variety of disciplines. A number of important survey questions are sufficiently embarrassing, threatening, or incriminating that concern over response bias, protection of the privacy of respondents, and the vulnerability of the researcher to possible attempts to appropriate the data for nonresearch purposes suggests that the randomized response method be given serious consideration in future survey efforts.

APPENDIX:
INSTRUCTIONS TO RESPONDENTS

In any survey effort, promoting respondent cooperation through clear and convincing instructions and guarantees of protection is fundamentally critical. In a randomized response survey, moreover, the combination of a sensitive or threatening focus of inquiry with a seemingly bizarre procedure mandates close attention to designing instructions that will engender respondent comfort and confidence rather than suspicion and distrust. (The additional requirement of hiring and training interviewers who can carry off the delicate procedure is beyond the scope of this discussion.)

There are, unfortunately, no standard phrases that we can suggest for all situations. Of course, the manner in which one introduces and explains the technique will depend on the particular form of randomized response to be used. Nevertheless, we can provide two sets of instructions—one for the qualitative case and one for the quantitative case—that we have found to work successfully in surveys utilizing randomized response.

Figure A.1 reproduces a randomized response item concerning weapons possession from a survey of violence, fear, and discipline in the Boston public high schools (Fox, 1983). Though dealing with a difficult population of inner-city adolescents, we found most respondents to follow—if not understand—the procedure.

One frequent occurrence is noteworthy. A small, but nontrivial, proportion of respondents, when confronted with the randomized response procedure, said in effect, "I don't need this coin thing; I'll just tell you the answer." In such instances, the interviewers made a notation of this reaction. Then, in estimating the prevalence of weapons possession, these observations were handled in the standard (direct inquiry) way. (As it happened, the estimated prevalence for both those who followed the procedure and those who insisted on responding directly was in the neighborhood of 30 percent.)

Figure A.2 displays the randomized response portion of an interview schedule used in a validation study on a sample of Philadelphians having prior arrest records (Tracy and Fox, 1981). (The respondents were unaware that we knew of and had copies of their rap sheets.) Although former arrestees in an urban setting would seem to present a difficult population to survey in this manner, the procedure worked well in the field, at least according to the interview staff.

31. I'd like to ask you about whether you have ever had a weapon at school, but I don't want to put you on the spot. So I will use a procedure that will protect your answer and make it perfectly safe for you to answer.

First, without telling me it, think of the month that your (FILL IN RELATIVE FROM Q. 29) birthday is in. (MAKE CERTAIN THAT RESPONDENT KNOWS THIS PERSON'S BIRTH MONTH; IF NOT, ASK ABOUT ANOTHER RELATIVE.)

I will be giving you two questions, but you only answer one of them depending on what you get when you flip a coin. Even though I will hear the answer you give, I will not know what question you are answering. Thus, I will not know whether you personally carry a weapon, but it will help us to understand how common weapons are in this school.

HAND RESPONDENT CARD C AND A COIN

CARD C

HEAD: Have you carried or kept a weapon at school this year? Yes or No

TAIL: Is this person's birthday in December?   Yes or No

Without telling me what you get, you will flip the coin.

If you get a head, answer yes or no to the question:

   Have you carried or kept a weapon at school this year?

If you get a tail, answer yes or no to the question:

   Is this person's birthday in December?

Now without telling me what you get on the coin flip, please flip the coin and answer the question called for by "yes" or "no," but do not tell me the question that you are answering.

RESPONSE: YES   1
               NO   2

SOURCE: Fox (1983).

Figure A.1: Instructions for a Qualitative Response

Among the field procedures, a pad of paper proved particularly useful. Since the respondent was instructed to provide either an answer to a question or read a digit off of a ball, any delay in the response would suggest to the interviewer that it was an artificial one. To prevent this, all respondents were directed first to write down on a pad of paper his or her would-be answer to the sensitive

- In this container there are an equal number of red and white balls. The white balls all have numbers printed upon them. As you can see, the numbers range from zero to eight. By tilting the container, one ball drops into the neck.

- I will be asking you a few questions. If a white ball is chosen, answer my question by telling me the number printed on the ball. If a red ball is chosen tell me the correct answer to the question. (DEMONSTRATE EACH COLOR)

- I will place a barrier between us so that I can't see which color ball is selected.

- (PRESENT SAMPLE CARD AND ANSWER PAPER) Let us go through an example. Read the question on this card. How many days in the last eight days have you eaten dinner in a restaurant?

- Without telling me the answer, write the number on this piece of paper. The answer should be a number such as zero, one, two, three and so on.

- Turn the container over a few times to mix up the balls. Then tilt it forward so that a ball drops into the neck. Remember that if the ball is white, read the number on the ball. If the ball is red, read the number on your paper.

- This time you have turned up a (COLOR) ball. Going by this color, tell me what your answer would be to the question, "How many days in the last eight days have you eaten dinner in a restaurant?" (BE SURE ANSWER IS APPROPRIATE TO THE COLOR OF THE BALL). Now suppose that you turned up a (OPPOSITE COLOR) ball. Then what would your answer be?

- Always give your answer in numbers, such as zero, one, two, and so on. Avoid using words like none or once so that I can't tell whether you are reading the number on the ball or answering the question.

- By using this method, neither I nor anyone else will ever know if the number you provide is the real answer to the question or the number printed on the ball. It is used to protect your privacy. The answer will, however, help us to understand the entire sample as a group. The information you provide will not tell anything about you personally.

- Now we are ready to begin.

SOURCE: Fox and Tracy (1980a).

Figure A.2: Instructions for a Quantitative Response *(continued)*

PUT THE BARRIER IN PLACE. HAND CARDS TO RESPONDENT ONE AT A TIME.
READ QUESTION. Let's go over the steps again:

- Mix the balls well

- Write the correct answer to the question on a piece of paper

- Tilt the container until a ball comes to the neck

- If red ball -- tell me correct answer from piece of paper
  If white ball -- tell me number on ball

- Destroy piece of paper after each question

(10.) First, how many magazines and newspapers do you subscribe to?

ENTER #:_____

(11.) How many days in the last eight days have you had an alcoholic beverage?

ENTER #:_____

(12.) In the last two years, how many automobile speeding tickets have you received?

ENTER #:_____

(13.) Since the age of 18, how many times have you been arrested and booked in a Philadelphia police station? That includes being fingerprinted, having your picture taken, etc. Please tell me the number of arrests by Philadelphia police only.

ENTER #:_____

(14.) Since the age of 18, what is the number of times you have been convicted in a Philadelphia court for any crime?

ENTER #:_____

(15.) In the last year, what is the number of times you have been physically assaulted?

ENTER #:_____

Figure A.2 Continued

question, and only then to manipulate the device and respond accordingly. In one interesting case the respondent, after completing the series of randomized inquiries, insisted on destroying not only the used slips of paper but several sheets underneath that might hold an impression. It is indeed this type of suspicious respondent for whom randomized response is ideally suited and direct questioning is bound to fail.

NOTES

1. Although these topics are usually included in texts on research methods and research design, their coverage is limited. Work by Bradburn and Sudman (1979) and Sudman and Bradburn (1982), for example, reflects the concern that survey methods require more in-depth coverage than has been the case in the past.

2. For some early statements on the problem of response error, see Hansen et al. (1951), Madou (1965), and Magnusson (1966). More recent expositions of the topic can be found in Sudman and Bradburn (1974) and Cannell et al. (1977a, 1977b).

3. The ethical issues that arise from research with human subjects are not new. However, the social science literature shows a dearth of comprehensive treatments of the problems and possible solutions. A major exception is the work by Boruch and Cecil (1979). In this section we have drawn heavily on their ideas. The reader is referred to the original work for a superb discussion of many of the issues reviewed briefly here.

4. For example, the structure of a self-administered questionnaire must be simple enough for the respondent to follow. Thus complex branchings, probes, and open-ended questions are to be avoided.

5. A 20 percent chance of not firing a bullet may not always be sufficient protection for the shooters, thereby encouraging a marksman to shoot purposely off-target so that another of the shooters will fire the fatal bullet. In the 1951 execution of Elisio J. Mares, Utah correctional officials were embarrassed when all four bullets missed the cloth target placed over the condemned man's heart; four bullets penetrated the right side of Mares's chest, killing him, though neither instantaneously nor painlessly.

6. For the purposes of this illustration we shall ignore the obvious nonrepresentativeness of any such gathering, be it a lodge meeting or a PTA meeting.

7. As a practical note, one should instruct the respondent to write down his or her answer to the sensitive question on a slip of paper (to be discarded afterward) before rolling the die. Otherwise, any delay in responding may suggest to the interviewer that the respondent's roll directed him or her to answer the threatening question.

8. This is meant in strictly a statistical sense in terms of the conditional probability of the sensitive attribute given a "yes" response. In a sociological sense, the rarer sensitive behaviors are often those that are most taboo and thus more stigmatizing.

9. If one is too strict in setting minimally allowable levels of these factors, no suitable combination of values of p and π_y may result.

10. The logic of the sums approach was present in an earlier, yet more compelx, design called "block total response" (see Raghavarao and Federer, 1979).

11. Drane (1976) proved that the independence of the undelying traits implies independence of the observed responses, as well as the converse.

12. This study could be considered validational, since it compares randomized response estimates to known values. In the absence of a comparison to any competing technique, however, we prefer not to classify it as a true validation and thus include it here.

13. This passage reproduced with permission of the authors.

REFERENCES

ABERNATHY, J. R., B. G. GREENBERG, and D. G. HORVITZ (1970) "Estimates of induced abortion in urban North Carolina." Demography 7: 19-29.

ABUL-ELA, A. L. A., B. G. GREENBERG, and D. G. HORVITZ (1967) "A multiproportions randomized response model." Journal of the American Statistical Association 62: 990-1008.

ASTIN, A. W. and R. R. BORUCH (1970) "A link file system for assuring confidentiality of research data in longitudinal studies." American Educational Research Journal 7: 615-624.

BOURKE, P. D. (1974) "Symmetry of response in randomized response designs." Report No. 76 of the research project, Errors in Surveys. Stockholm: University of Stockholm, Institute of Statistics.

BOURKE, P. D. and T. DALENIUS (1975) "Some new ideas in the realm of randomized inquiries." Report No. 5 of the research project, Confidentiality in Surveys. Stockholm: University of Stockholm, Institute of Statistics.

———(1973) "Multi-proportions randomized response using a single sample. Report No. 68 of the research project, Errors in Surveys. Stockholm: University of Stockholm, Institute of Statistics.

BORUCH, R. F. (1972) "Relations among statistical methods for assuring confidentiality of social research data." Social Science Research 1: 403-414.

———(1971) "Assuring confidentiality of responses in social research: A note on strategies." American Sociologist 6: 308-311.

———and J. S. CECIL (1979) Assuring the Confidentiality of Social Research Data. Philadelphia: University of Pennsylvania Press.

BRADBURN, N. M. and S. SUDMAN (1979) Improving Interview Method and Questionnaire Design. San Francisco: Jossey-Bass.

BRIDGES, G. S. (1979) "Levels of effects of response error in self-reports of crime and delinquency." Ph.D. dissertation, University of Pennsylvania.

BROWN, G. H. and F. D. HARDING (1973) "A comparison of methods of studying illicit drug usage." HUMRO Technical Report 73-9. Alexandria, VA: Human Resources Research Organization.

BROWN, G. H. (1975) "Randomized inquiry vs. conventional questionnaire methods in estimating drug usage rates through mail surveys." HUMRO Technical Report 75-14. Alexandria, VA: Human Resources Research Organization.

CANNELL, C. F., K. H. MARQUIS, and A. LAURENT (1977) "A summary of studies of interviewing methodology." Vital and Health Statistics, Series 2, No. 69. Rockville, MD: U.S. National Center for Health Statistics.

CANNELL, C. F., L. OKSENBERG, and J. CONVERSE (1977) "Experiments in interviewing techniques." NCHSR Report 78-7. Hyattsville, MD: National Center for Health Services Research.

CHEN, T. T. (1979) "Analysis of randomized response as purposively misclassified data." Proceedings of the Survey Research Methods Section, American Statistical Association.

———(1978) "Log-linear models for the categorical data obtained from randomized response techniques." Proceedings of the Social Statistics Section, American Statistical Association.

DAWES, R. M. (1974) "Guttman scaling randomized responses: A technique for evaluating the underlying structures of behaviors to which people may not wish to admit." University of Oregon, Oregon Research Institute (mimeo).

DRANE, W. (1976) "On the theory of randomized response to two sensitive questions." Communications in Statistics: Theory and Methods 5: 565-574.

DURHAM, A. M. and M. J. LICHTENSTEIN (1983) "Response bias in self-report surveys: Evaluation of randomized responses," in G. P. Waldo (ed.) Measurement Issues in Criminal Justice. Beverly Hills, CA: Sage.

EDGELL, S. E., S. HIMMELFARB, and K. L. DUCHAN (1982) "The validity of forced responses in a randomized response model." Sociological Methods and Research 11: 89-100.

FOLSOM, R. E. (1974) "A randomized response validation study: Comparison of direct and randomized reporting of DUI arrests." Final Report 2550-807. Chapel Hill, NC: Research Triangle Institute.

———B. G. GREENBERG, D. G. HORVITZ, and J. R. ABERNATHY (1973) "The two alternate questions randomized response model for human surveys." Journal of the American Statistical Association 68: 525-530.

FOX, J. A. (1983) "Victimization, fear, and discipline in four Boston public high schools." Report to the Boston Safe Schools Commission, Northeastern University (mimeo).

FOX, J. A. and P. E. TRACY (1986) "Indeterminate response: a simplified alternative to randomized response." Northeastern University (mimeo).

FOX, J. A. and P. E. TRACY (1984) "Measuring associations with randomized response." Social Science Research 13: 188-197.

FOX, J. A. and P. E. TRACY (1980a) "A Comparative validation of the randomized response and direct question methods." Final report to the National Institute of Law Enforcement and Criminal Justice, Washington, DC.

FOX, J. A. and P. E. TRACY (1980b) "The randomized response approach: Applicability to criminal justice research evaluation." Evaluation Review 4: 601-622.

GEURTS, M. D., R. R. ANDRUS, and J. REINMUTH (1975) "Researching shoplifting and other deviant customer behavior using the randomized research design." Journal of Retailing 51: 43-48.

GOODSTADT, M. S. and V. GRUSON (1975) "The randomized response technique: A test on drug use." Journal of the American Statistical Association 70: 814-818.

GREENBERG, B. G., J. R. ABERNATHY, and D. G. HORVITZ (1970) "A new survey technique and its application in the field of public health." Milbank Memorial Fund Quarterly 68: 39-55.

GREENBERG, B. G., R. R. KEUBLER, J. R. ABERNATHY, and D. G. HORVITZ (1977) "Respondent hazards in the unrelated question randomized response model." Journal of Statistical Planning and Inference 1: 53-60.

———(1971) "Application of the randomized response technique in obtaining quantitative data." Journal of the American Statistical Association 66: 243-250.

HANSEN, M. H., W. N. HURWITZ, E. S. MARKS, and W. P. MAUDLIN (1951) "Response error in surveys." Journal of the American Statistical Association 46: 147-190.

HARDT, R. H. and S. PETERSON-HARDT (1977) "On determining the quality of the delinquency self-report method." Journal of Research in Crime and Delinquency 14: 247-261.

HIMMELFARB, S. and S. E. EDGELL (1980) "Additive constants model: A randomized response technique for eliminating evasiveness to quantitative response questions." Psychological Bulletin 87: 525-530.

HIMMELFARB, S. and C. LICKSTEIG (1982) "Social desirability and the randomized response technique." Journal of Personality and Social Psychology 43: 710-717.

HORVITZ, D. G., B. U. SHAH, and W. R. SIMMONS (1967) "The unrelated question randomized response model." Proceedings of the Social Statistics Section, American Statistical Association.

I-CHENG, C., L. P. CHOW, and R. V. RIDER (1972) "The randomized response technique as used in the Taiwan outcome of pregnancy study." Studies in Family Planning 2: 265-269.

IIT Research Institute (1971) A Study of Organized Crime in Illinois. Chicago: Chicago Crime Commission.

KROTKI, K. and B. FOX (1974) "The randomized response technique, the interview, and the self-administered questionnaire: An empirical comparison of fertility reports." Proceedings of the Social Statistics Section, American Statistical Association.

LAMB, C. W. and D. E. STEM (1978) "An empirical validation of the randomized response technique." Journal of Marketing Research 15: 616-621.

LANKE, J. (1975) "On the choice of the unrelated question in Simmons' version of randomized response." Journal of the American Statistical Association 70: 80-83.

LEYSIEFFER, F. W. (1975) "Respondent jeopardy in randomized response procedures." Florida State University Statistics Report M338.

——and S. L. WARNER (1976) "Respondent jeopardy and optimal designs in randomized response models." Journal of the American Statistical Association 71: 649-656.

LIU, P. T. and L. P. CHOW (1976a) "A new discrete quantitative randomized response model." Journal of the American Statistical Association 71: 72-73.

LIU, P. T. and L. P. CHOW (1976b) "The efficiency of the multiple trial randomized response technique." Biometrics 32: 607-618.

LOCANDER, W., S. SUDMAN, and N. M. BRADBURN (1976) "An investigation of interview method, threat, and response distortion." Journal of the American Statistical Association 71: 269-275.

MADIGAN, F. C., J. R. ABERNATHY, A. N. HERRIN, and C. TAN (1975) "Purposive treatment concealment of death in household surveys in Misamus Oriental Province." Mindanao Center for Population Studies (mimeo).

MADOW, W. (1965) "On some aspects of response error measurement." Proceedings of the Social Statistics Section, American Statistical Association.

MAGNUSSON, D. F. (1966) Test Theory. Reading, MA: Addison-Wesley.

MILLER, J. D. (1984) "A new survey technique for studying deviant behavior." Unpublished Ph.D. dissertation, George Washington University. Department of Sociology.

MILLER, J. D., and I. H. CISIN (1984) "The item-count/paired lists technique: An indirect method of surveying deviant behavior." Unpublished manuscript, George Washington University, Social Research Group (mimeo).

MOORS, J.J.A. (1971) "Optimization of the unrelated question randomized response model." Journal of the American Statistical Association 66: 627-629.

MORIARTY, M. and F. WISEMAN (1976) "On the choice of a randomization technique with the randomized response model." Proceedings of the Social Statistics Section of the American Statistical, Association.

National Academy of Sciences (1979) Report of the Panel on Privacy and Confidentiality as Factors in Survey Response. Washington, DC: NAS.

PHILLIPS, D. L. (1971) Knowledge from What? Chicago: Rand-McNally.

RAGHAVARAO, D. and W. T. FEDERER (1979) "Block total response as an alternative to the randomized response method in surveys." Journal of the Royal Statistical Society, Series B, 41: 40-45.

REASER, J. M., S. HARTSOCK, and A. J. HOEHN (1975) "A test of the forced-alternative randomized response questionnaire technique." HUMRO Technical Report 75-9. Alexandria, VA: Human Resources Research Organization.

ROSENBERG, M. J. (1980) "Categorical data analysis by a randomized response technique for statistical disclosure control." Proceedings of the Survey Research Section, American Statistical Association.

———(1979) "Multivariable analysis by a randomized response technique for disclosure control." Ph.D. Dissertation, University of Michigan.

SHIMIZU, I. M. and G. S. BONHAM (1978) "Randomized response technique in a national survey." Journal of the American Statistical Association 73: 35-39.

STEM, D. E. and R. K. STEINHORST (1984) "Telephone interview and mail questionnaire applications of the randomized response model." Journal of the American Statistical Association 79: 555-564.

SUDMAN, S. and N. M. BRADBURN (1982) Asking Questions: A Practical Guide to Questionnaire Design. San Francisco: Jossey-Bass.

———(1974) Response Effects in Surveys: A Review and Synthesis. Chicago: Aldine.

TRACY, P. E. and J. A. FOX (1981) "The validity of randomized response for sensitive measurements." American Sociological Review 46: 187-200.

WARNER, S. L. (1965) "Randomized response: A survey technique for eliminating evasive answer bias." Journal of the American Statistical Association 60: 63-69.

WEIS, J. G. and D. V. ALSTYNE (1979) "The measurement of delinquency by the randomized response method." Presented at the annual meeting of the American Society of Criminology.

ZDEP, S. M. and I. N. RHODES (1976) "Making the randomized response technique work." Public Opinion Quarterly 40: 531-537.

JAMES ALAN FOX *is Professor of Criminal Justice at Northeastern University in Boston. His research generally involves the analysis of crime statistics, and his most recent book, co-authored with Jack Levin, is* Mass Murder: America's Growing Menace *(Plenum, 1985). He is Editor of the* Journal of Quantitative Criminology.

PAUL E. TRACY *is Assistant Professor and Director of the Graduate Program in Criminal Justice at Northeastern University in Boston. His primary research interests include the longitudinal study of delinquency and the prediction of adult criminality. He is co-author, with Marvin Wolfgang and Robert Figlio, of* Delinquency in Two Birth Cohorts *and* The National Survey of Crime Severity.

Quantitative Applications in the Social Sciences

A SAGE UNIVERSITY PAPERS SERIES

$9.75 each

Place
Stamp
here

SAGE PUBLICATIONS, INC.
P.O. BOX 5084
THOUSAND OAKS, CALIFORNIA 91359-9924